OCS Study
MMS 2004-040

Strong Mid-Depth Currents and a Deep Cyclonic Gyre in the Gulf of Mexico

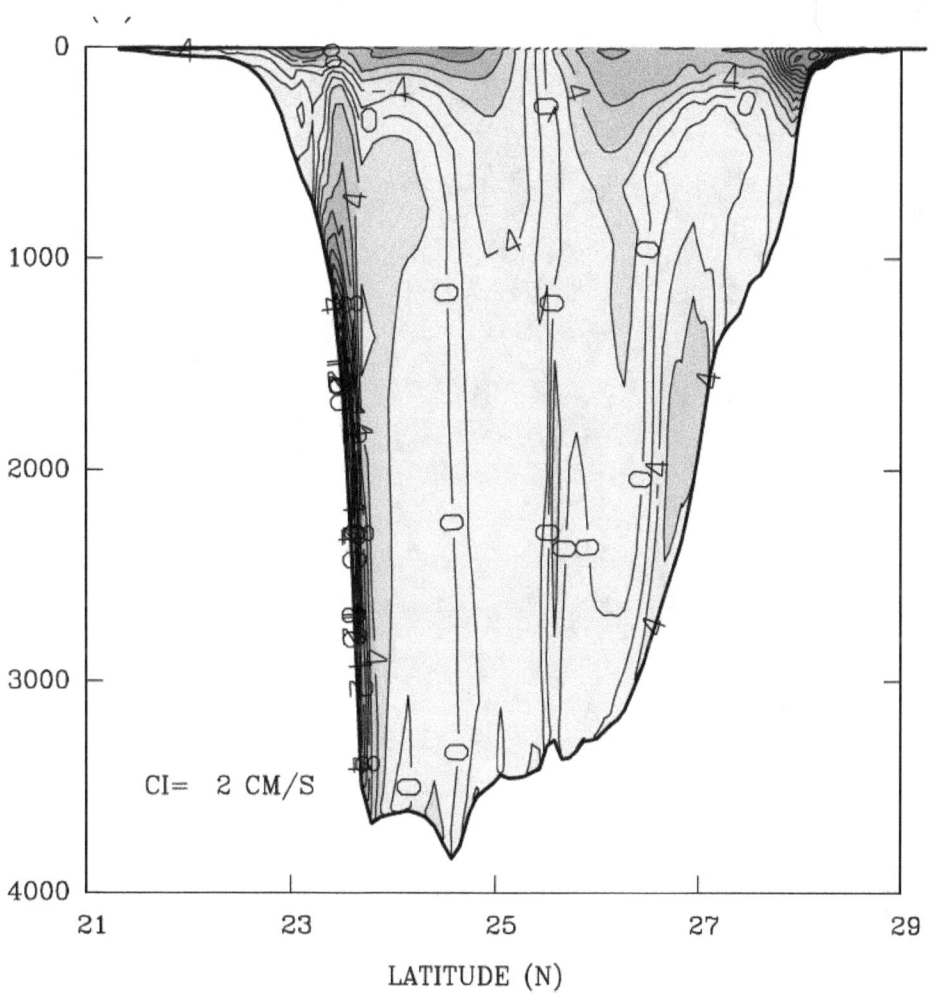

MMS U.S. Department of the Interior
Minerals Management Service
Gulf of Mexico OCS Region

OCS Study
MMS 2004-040

Strong Mid-Depth Currents and a Deep Cyclonic Gyre in the Gulf of Mexico

Authors

Wilton Sturges
Department of Oceanography
Florida State University
Tallahassee, Florida

Eric Chassignet
RSMAS
University of Miami
Miami, Florida

Tal Ezer
Atmospheric & Oceanic Sciences
Princeton University
Princeton, New Jersey

Prepared under MMS Contract
14-35-01-99-CT-31027
by
Florida State University
Department of Oceanography
Tallahassee, Florida

Published by

U.S. Department of the Interior
Minerals Management Service
Gulf of Mexico OCS Region

New Orleans
May 2004

DISCLAIMER

This report was prepared under contract between the Minerals Management Service (MMS) and Florida State University (FSU). This report has been technically reviewed by MMS, and it has been approved for publication. Approval does not signify that the contents necessarily reflect the views and policies of MMS, nor does mention of trade names or commercial products constitute endorsement or recommendation for use. It is, however, exempt from review and compliance with MMS editorial standards.

REPORT AVAILABILITY

Extra copies of the report may be obtained from the Public Information Office (Mail Stop 5034) at the following address:

U.S. Department of the Interior
Minerals Management Service
Gulf of Mexico OCS Region
Public Information Office (MS 5034)
1201 Elmwood Park Boulevard
New Orleans, LA 70123-2394
Telephone: 1-800-200-GULF or
504-736-2519

CITATION

Suggested citation:

Sturges, W., E. Chassignet, and T. Ezer. 2004. Strong mid-depth currents and a deep cyclonic gyre in the Gulf of Mexico: Final report. U.S. Dept. of the Interior, Minerals Management Service, Gulf of Mexico OCS Region, New Orleans, LA. OCS Study MMS 2004-040. 89 pp.

ABOUT THE COVER

The cover figure shows a vertical section at 90°W in the Gulf of Mexico; the contours are the mean E-W velocity from the Princeton model. The deep mean flow along the northern (U.S.) side is now well documented. The prominent feature along the southern (Mexican) side shows deep flow to the east. That eastward-flowing current has not been observed but is predicted by the studies in this report.

ACKNOWLEDGMENTS

We thank Evans Waddell and Peter Hamilton, SAIC, Inc., Raleigh NC for generously providing us with data of various kinds and on many occasions. We thank our colleagues G. L. Weatherly and N. Wienders (F.S.U.) for allowing us the use of the early, unpublished results of their corrected float data from the NOPP program early on in our work. We thank David Szabo of Fugro GEOS for allowing us limited access to proprietary data from the GULL program. We thank Ms. Jane Jimeian for help with the data analysis and Mrs. E. Shargel for editorial assistance and advice.

During the course of this work, Chassignet was assisted by Dr. Anastasia Romanou and Dr. Laurent Cherubin; Sturges was assisted by Dr. Christopher J. DeHaan. We have had the good fortune to have the excellent assistance of both Dr. Carole Current and Dr. Alexis Lugo-Fernandez as the MMS Contracting Officer's Technical Representatives. It is a pleasure to acknowledge our gratitude for their cooperation and assistance.

TABLE OF CONTENTS

LIST OF FIGURES

LIST OF FIGURES
(continued)

LIST OF TABLES

1.   EXECUTIVE SUMMARY

The main purpose of this work was to explore the possibility that the deep flow (~2000 m) around the edges of the Gulf circulates in a cyclonic, or counter-clockwise direction. The existence of such flow was proposed on theoretical grounds but had not been previously documented. Our results are quite clear that such flow is reliably observed.

Recall that the surface flow in the eastern Gulf is strongly anticyclonic as a result of the Loop Current. The surface flow in the western Gulf is also largely anticyclonic as a result of both wind forcing and the presence of large eddies that separate from the Loop Current. So a cyclonic deep flow might appear at first glance to be counter-intuitive. One tacit over-simplification we have made is that the deep flow in both the eastern and western Gulf can be adequately described as a simple large gyre. We suspect that better measurements in the future will lead to an awareness of a richer mean field with more detail, but at the moment the database is not sufficient to allow better resolution. It should be clear that, being strictly a boundary flow, there is ample space for a much more detailed flow in the interior.

Surprisingly, the warm-core temperature and density patterns associated with these surface flows extend to at least 2000 m. There are reasons, however, to suspect that the deep mean flow should actually be cyclonic. Topographic wave rectification and vortex stretching contribute to this cyclonic tendency, as will the supply of cold incoming deep water at the edges of the basin. We find that the deep mean flow is cyclonic both in the eastern and western Gulf, with speeds on the order of 2 to 4 cm/s at 2000 m. Recent observations at deep moorings in the northern Gulf reveal even stronger mean speeds.

This report is based on observational and numerical modeling studies and it deals with three separate but related topics. The observations include four separate groups of current-meter moorings at different locations and in different years. The observations range in duration from nearly one year to three years. There was also a major deep-drifting buoy project in the western Gulf that gave supportive results. While this was hypothesized from a theoretical point of view, the conclusive evidence is completely observational. This cyclonic mean deep flow takes place around the edges of the basin, rather like the well-known deep western boundary current off the east coast of the U.S. We are not aware of any long-term data set that offers conflicting evidence.

The temperature around the edges of the basin at 2000 m is coldest near Yucatan Channel, where Caribbean Sea water is colder by ~0.1°C. The temperature increases steadily with distance from Yucatan in the counter-clockwise direction, consistent with a deep mean cyclonic boundary flow.

The second purpose of the work was to try to explain the rare but persistent findings of strong bursts of flow at intermediate depths, as reported by drilling platform operators. It is possible to search for such bursts of flow in the results from numerical models. The models used here are two of the best-known models in oceanography: The Princeton Ocean Model, which is an outgrowth of the Mellor-Yamada model, and the Miami Isopycnic Coordinate Model, or MICOM. Some strong bursts of flow are found, as reported herein, but while the results are informative, they are not compelling. One fundamental difficulty is that the reported observations of these strong flows continue to be remarkably elusive, so it is difficult to know exactly what one should be looking for in the models and under what conditions.

The third part of our results deals with comparisons between the observations and the numerical modeling results. At this stage in numerical model development, results tend to capture most of the major time-dependent features of ocean circulation rather well. However the mean flows over many years are perhaps not the most reliable part of the results. The interesting result here is that, when two "top of the line" numerical models were run by experienced practitioners, one of the models found a deep mean flow that is consistent with the observations, and the other model did not. And the reasons for the differences are the subject of considerable debate. It obviously will require further study to help unravel this mystery. Figure 1.1, which also appears on the cover of this report, is a N-S section through the Gulf at 90° W. Mexico is on the left, the U.S. on the right. The region of flow of ~4 cm/sec (to the west) along the steep slope off the U.S. coast, at depths of 1500-2500 m, was found to be quite consistent with two separate long-term current-meter mooring arrays. The observations of this flow are discussed in Section 3 and the numerical modeling in Section 4.

It is appropriate to point out the significance of the primary finding of this work. The deep mean cyclonic flow in the Gulf appears to be analogous in many ways to the deep western boundary current of North Atlantic Deep Water flowing to the south along the east coasts of North and South America. The deep flow in the Gulf is strongly time-dependent; its cyclonic nature emerges primarily in the time mean, as the instantaneous velocities have a large standard deviation. Our understanding of deep western boundary flows in general is that the source regions

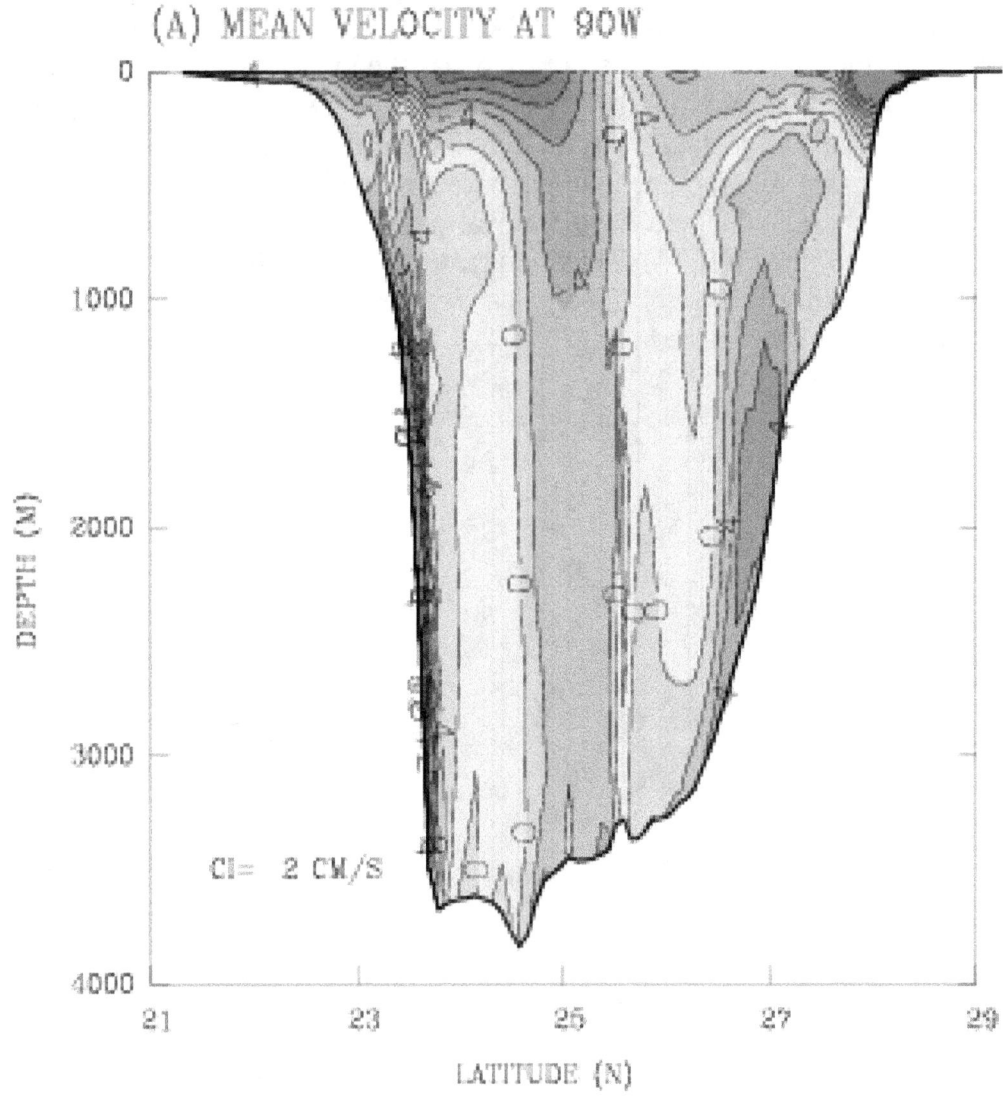

Figure 1.1. Mean East-West velocity component along a North-South section at 90° W from the Princeton Ocean Model. The mean speed over 5 years is shown in cm/sec.

of cold deep water are in the far north and the cold water flows generally to the south. Because there is such large eddy variability, the cold source waters slowly bleed off into the interior by eddy fluxes as the main body of flow continues south. The cold signal is continually but slowly eroded away. These eddy processes have not been studied extensively in the Gulf, and are not the subject of our study here. The main point of course is that these results suggest both a mechanism and a pathway whereby the cold deep renewal water from the Caribbean is supplied to the interior of the Gulf. These added features are based on the analogy with deep western boundary currents. They have not yet been observed or studied in the Gulf and remain to be explored further.

2. INTRODUCTION

2.1. Introduction

The Loop Current and the warm-core rings that detach from it dominate the upper-layer flow in the Gulf of Mexico. The well-known primary flow enters the Caribbean Sea from the open Atlantic, flows into the Gulf of Mexico through Yucatan Channel and leaves the Gulf to form the Florida Current and Gulf Stream (see, for example, Schmitz and Richardson, 1991; Niiler and Richardson, 1973). There have been several earlier attempts to summarize the flow in the Gulf using the historical data (see Hoffman and Worley, 1986; Molinari et al., 1978). The upper-layer flow has been observed fairly well in recent years by satellite observations of temperature and sea-surface height. The main flow is restricted to approximately 850 m as a result of the limiting depth of the Florida Straits.

The deep flow has been described by Hamilton (1990). A magnificent new set of mooring data in the Yucatan Channel has now been reported (Bunge et al., 2002; Ochoa et al., 2001; Sheinbaum et al. 2002). The mean upper-layer flow is well described by almost any temperature or density surface near or in the main thermocline. Figure 2.1 shows an attempt to determine the (long-term) mean temperature at 400 m. The mean depth of the 27.0-sigma-t surface shows a similar structure. The dots that appear to be data points are local means of essentially random concentrations of ~5-10 hydro stations. Using data from many years, these were selected from the full historical NODC data base (Conkright et al., 2000) in an attempt to suppress the very great time variability of warm-core rings propagating to the west.

Two individual warm-core features are evident in Figure 2.1. Although the Loop Current position is notoriously variable, it is well known that a clear mean emerges in the east . In the central and western Gulf the anticyclonic pattern is maintained both by the mean wind field and by the passage of large warm-core rings that have separated from the Loop Current. The relative importance of these two forcing mechanisms remains an open question. The western gyre appears to have southerly flow from ~90°W to ~95°W; the models used here generally show this flow (plus details; see for example the maps of velocity at 400 m, Figure 4.1, *et seq.,* later in this report). At the far western edge, however, the strong core of northerly flow found in the models is not apparent in the data as a result of poor data resolution. One problem has been that the majority of the older hydro

5

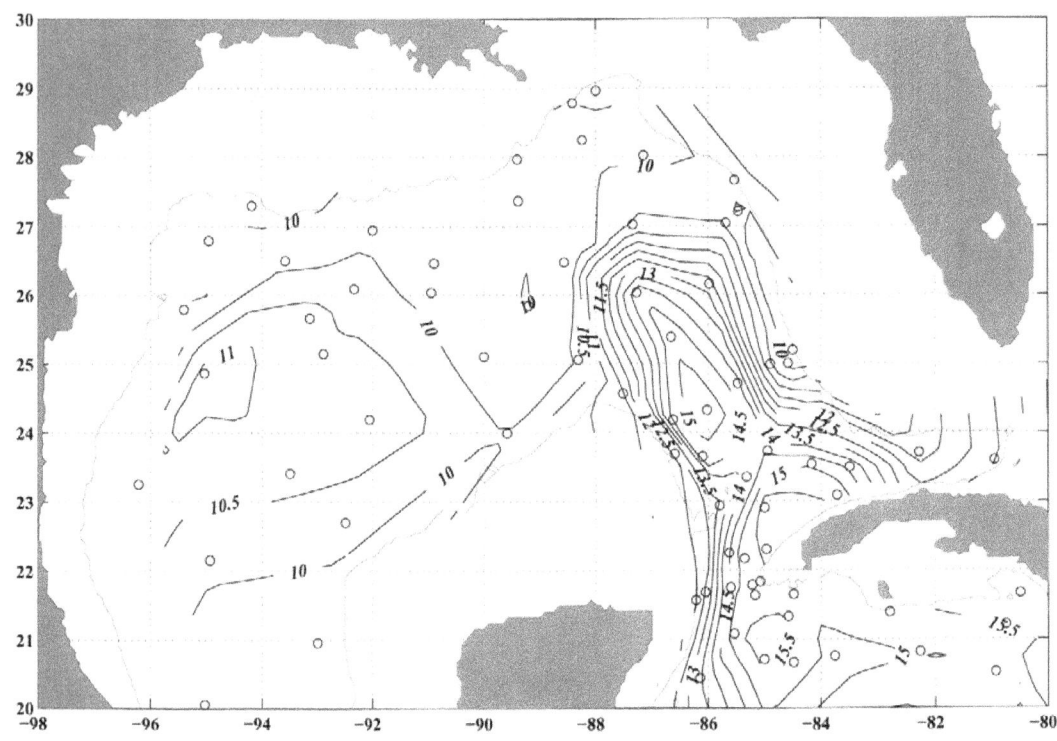

Figure 2.1. Time-mean temperature distribution at 400 m, based on the full
historical database from NODC. The individual dots that appear to be
data points are local means computed from ~5-10 hydro stations
concentrated near the point. The 1,000-m isobath is shown. The flow
between Cuba and Florida is not resolved in these data.

sections run N-S. Though we know the upper-layer flow fairly well, we do not know the deep flow very well at all. Several numerical models include the Gulf of Mexico, but good observations at depth are scarce. The intriguing fact is that the upper-layer flow, so obviously anticyclonic, appears to extend—in the density field—to depths of ~1,500 m to 2,000 m. Because we know that the flow in the Florida Current penetrates only to ~850 m we might expect the warm-core structure of Figure 2.1 to extend only to that depth, whereas observations show that it goes much deeper.

Figure 2.2 shows a map of temperature at 1,250 m. The warm-core patterns are still evident at this depth. They remain evident, if not as clearly so, as deep as 2,000 m. In the eastern Gulf, the horizontal temperature difference at 1,500 m is ~0.06° C between the central region and the eastern edge. In the central Gulf the difference has been eroded to ~0.04° C between the central region and the northern edge. This "temperature difference" signal is still evident at depths of 2,000 m. Table 2.1, adapted from DeHaan and Sturges (2004), shows the essential information.

Table 2.1

Mean Potential Temperature, °C, in the Centers and Edges of the
Eastern and Central Gulf of Mexico
(The first value is potential temperature; the second is the number of samples.)

	Central Warm Region	Outer Cool Region	Difference Δ T, °C
E. Gulf, 1,500 m	4.185, 44	4.130, 123	0.045
Central, 1,500 m	4.142, 32	4.105, 45	0.037
E. Gulf, 2,000 m	4.050, 19	4.016, 34	0.034
Central, 2,000 m	4.053, 21	4.024, 19	0.029

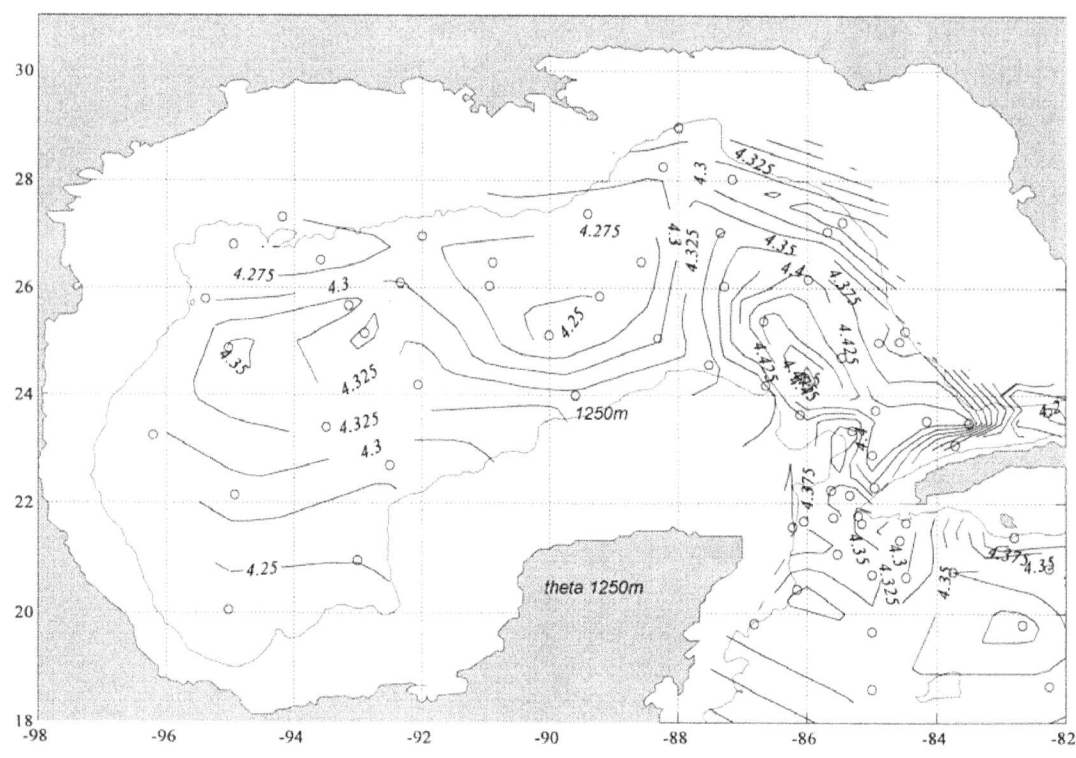

Figure 2.2. Time-mean distribution of potential temperature at 1,250 m relative to the sea surface, or 0 db. The original data set is the same as for Figure 2.1. The isobath shown is 1,250 m.

A "warm-core ring" in the upper ocean suggests anticyclonic flow, but (as is well known) in deep water this signal tells us only about vertical shear. For reasons put forth in the next section, it seems reasonable to expect that the deep mean flow should be *cyclonic*. And so we ask, is there evidence for a reversal of the mean flow between ~800 m and 1,500 m?

Some readers may raise the additional question: Why do we *care* about the direction of deep mean flow? Or, to put it another way, what is the significance of these results? The Caribbean Sea is the only source of deep water for the Gulf of Mexico, for no deep water is formed locally. The Caribbean source of cold deep water (e.g., Bunge et al., 2002) supplies oxygen and nutrients. The return flow flushes the deep Gulf. The deep mean cyclonic flow in the Gulf is analogous in many ways to the Deep Western Boundary Current of North Atlantic Deep Water flowing to the south along the east coasts of North and South America. The deep flow in the Gulf is strongly time-dependent; its cyclonic nature emerges primarily in the time mean, as the instantaneous velocities have a large standard deviation. Our understanding of deep western boundary flows in general is that the source regions of cold deep water are in high latitudes. In the case of NADW, the cold water flows generally to the south. Because there is such large eddy variability, the cold source waters slowly bleed off into the interior by eddy fluxes as the main body of flow continues south. The cold signal is continually but slowly eroded away. These eddy processes have not been studied extensively in the Gulf, and are not explored here. The main point of course is that these results point to a mechanism and a pathway whereby the cold deep renewal water from the Caribbean is supplied to the interior of the Gulf. These added features are based on the analogy with deep western boundary currents but have not been observed in the Gulf. These effects are obvious targets for further study if we are to understand the mixing of deep water and the residence times in the deep Gulf. Examples of such further questions would be, If a massive deep spill should occur, can we estimate the flushing time of the waters between 1,000 m and 2,000 m? Or at any depths?

2.2. Why We Expect the Deep Flow to be Cyclonic

There are three mechanisms here that could generate cyclonic deep flow. First, it is well known that there is a substantial amount of eddy-like activity over the entire basin at depth, composed mostly of topographic Rossby waves (Hamilton, 1990; Oey and Lee, 2002). Topographic rectification of these waves would contribute to cyclonic mean flow. Second, there is the introduction of cold deep water from the Caribbean, through the Yucatan Channel. At 2,000 m, the Caribbean is ~0.1° C cooler than the Gulf. Recent observations (e.g., Bunge et al., 2002) show that for intervals of many months the deep exchange can be as large as 5–10 Sv while the Loop Current goes through a ring-shedding cycle. Parcels of water would, of course, gradually lose their temperature deficit as they mix downstream from Yucatan. But we know from observations elsewhere (Mediterranean outflow, Denmark Straits overflow, Caribbean Sea inflow) that cold, dense incoming parcels hug the right-hand slope even after some mixing and sinking. This supply of cold dense water is analogous to, even if weaker than, the supply of North Atlantic Deep Water to the Deep Western Boundary current along the East coast of the United States. This effect also introduces colder water around the periphery, enhancing the existing "warm-core" shear structure.

A third mechanism, we suspect, operates only in the eastern Gulf. During one phase of the Loop Current cycle, as deep Caribbean waters flow over the sill into the Gulf, the "bottom falls away" in the downstream direction. Denser water that enters near 2,000 m flows into a weakly-stratified region where the bottom drops abruptly to ~3,500 m. The resultant vortex stretching should induce a cyclonic spin of the entering fluid, consistent with similar findings of Spall and Price (1998). By contrast, when water *leaves* the Gulf during the reverse phase of the Loop Current cycle, the ambient stratification in the Gulf, even though it is weak, tends to restrict the source of outgoing fluid to depths above the sill. So we expect much less vortex compression on the other half of the deep flow cycle.

3. ANALYSES OF AVAILABLE OBSERVATIONS

3.1. Deep Temperature Structure and Vertical Shear

3.1.1. Eastern Gulf

We have computed the vertical shear associated with these anticyclonic patterns. Figure 3.1 shows ten regions in which we computed the mean hydrographic conditions based on the available NODC database.

Because the variability is so great, we wished to use observations over as great a time span as possible and over as great a horizontal extent as seemed appropriate. From a construction of composite temperature-salinity curves we concluded that observations of temperature have much less apparent error, or scatter, than salinities. We also compared the temperature-salinity curves in various regions of the deep Gulf and could not convince ourselves that the t,S properties are significantly different from one region to another. For these reasons and because the salinity gradients are so small in the deep Gulf, we have chosen to compute density from a mean temperature-salinity curve, using the temperature data alone for gradient information. (For the reader interested in the details, Figure 3.14, at the end of this section, shows a plot of potential temperature against salinity for a collection of deep Gulf hydro stations.)

In the eastern Gulf, it turns out that the shear profile on the eastern side has a much better signal-to-noise ratio than that on the western side. The western side has sparse observations, contributing to the poor signal-to-noise ratio. The position of the Loop Current is constrained by the Florida shelf on the Eastern side, but not on the Western side, which may also contribute to the greater variability on the Western side.

Figure 3.2 shows the resulting mean temperature signal. Below 1,500 m, the standard deviation of the temperature variability is ~0.02°C in the central and eastern boxes; Figure 3.2 shows that the temperature differences are on the same order. (The standard error of the means, of course, is smaller.) We computed error estimates in the following way. Because the standard deviations of the temperature data values are as large as the signal, we estimated a standard error of the mean by computing the composite mean values between 1,000 and 2,000 m. The temperature difference on the eastern side was 0.13°C, with a standard error of the mean of 0.03°C, based on 106 observations in the east and 163 in the center.

11

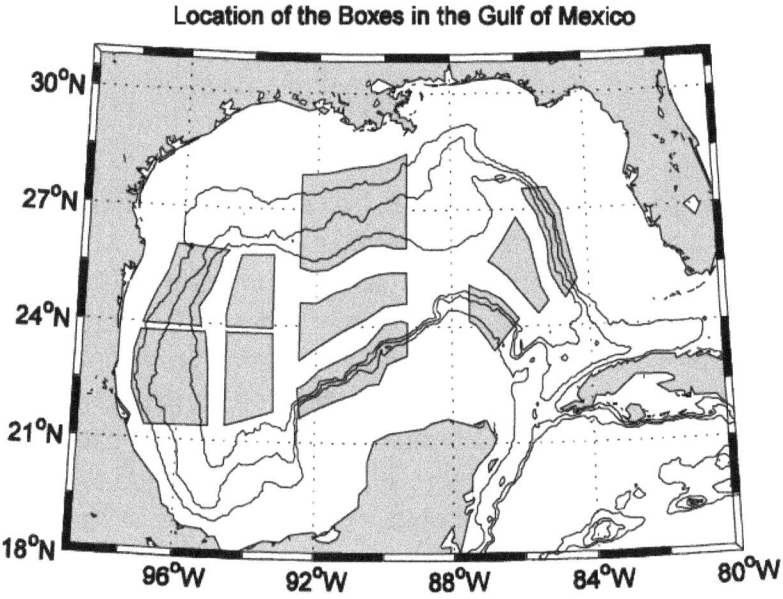

Figure 3.1. Location of the regions used to form data means for constructing shear profiles.

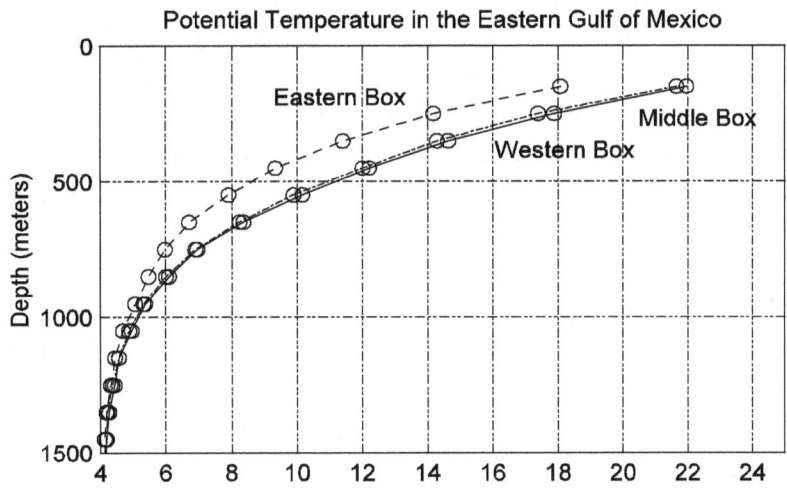

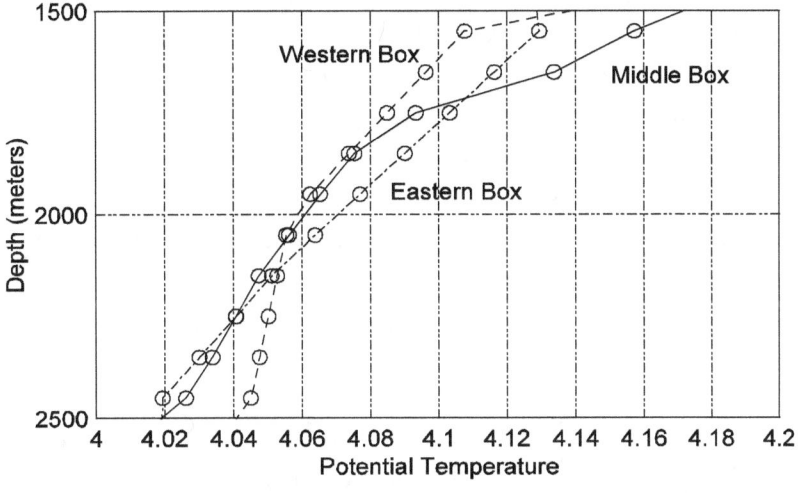

Figure 3.2. Mean vertical temperature distributions in the eastern Gulf of Mexico (an expanded scale is shown in the lower box). The regions used are shown in Figure 3.1.

We are not able to compute the *details* of the vertical shear with great accuracy, although the mean difference is reliably greater than the standard error. It should be emphasized, however, that the biggest variability in these data is not in the usual sense of "error," but *in time*. Multiple data points on a single hydro cast are not independent in the way we would like. The vertical averaging, however, will reduce problems from instrumental errors, internal waves, and other such sources. Therefore, the significance level is not nearly as high as one would like. Nevertheless, the same result holds true for all the individual calculations: the signals are small but consistently of the sign appropriate to support the idea of cyclonic flow. The geostrophic velocity computed from this temperature-density distribution is in Figure 3.3.

The flow at 2,000 m relative to 1,000 m is ~1 cm s^{-1} to the north. It is weak but reliably above the noise level. It remains, of course, to determine an appropriate but believable reference level for the geostrophic calculation. To anticipate the results of the next sections, however, we point out here that a 1,000-m reference level turns out to be a remarkably good choice.

The signal-to-noise ratio in our calculation is barely adequate on the east side beneath the Loop Current, but is even worse on the western side. The mean temperature difference there (between the central box and the western box, beneath the Loop Current – see Figure 3.1) is only 0.05°C and has a standard error of 0.04°C. There are a number of reasons why the computed signal could be so small. We are unable to offer any definitive explanation; beyond noting the fact that the data are quite sparse on the western side. The distribution of the number of stations *in the eastern region* (the region with more data), as shown in Figure 3.4, illustrates this problem nicely.

3.1.2. Central Gulf

In a fashion similar to our methods in the eastern Gulf, we have computed the mean geostrophic vertical shear in the central area of the Gulf using the regions shown in Figure 3.1. Figure 3.5 shows the velocity structure relative to 1000 m. The conventional velocity sign convention is used; "u" is positive east.

The deep velocity profile is shown for only the northern side of the Gulf because the signal-to-noise ratio is below the noise level on the southern side.

The flow at 2,000 m, relative to 1,000 m, is to the west in Figure 3.5, again suggesting a cyclonic flow pattern. (As before, the issue of justifying the choice of reference level is postponed to the next section.) The velocity at depth is only a

14

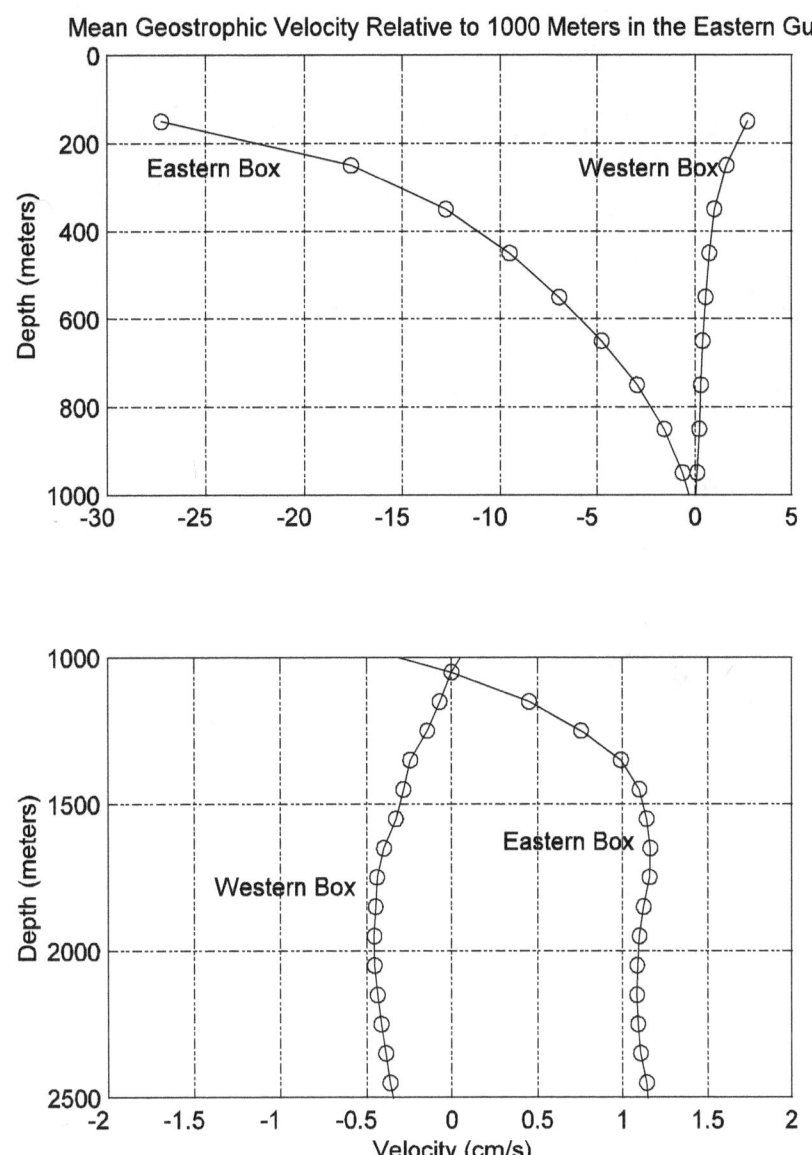

Figure 3.3. Mean N-S geostrophic speeds relative to 1,000 db computed from the temperature profiles of Figure 3.2 and using a mean T-S curve.

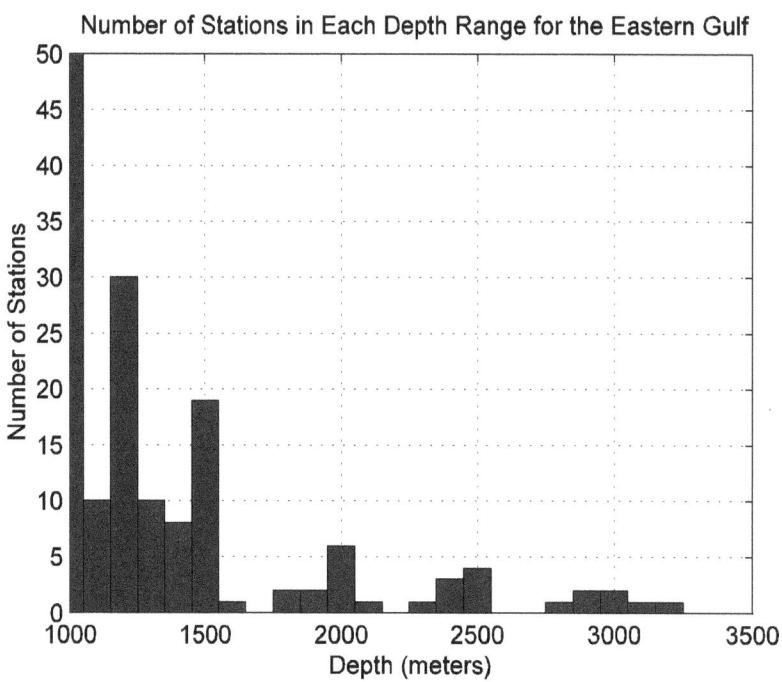

Figure 3.4. Histogram of the number of hydrographic observations at each depth for the eastern region (shown in Figure 3.1) of the eastern Gulf for these calculations.

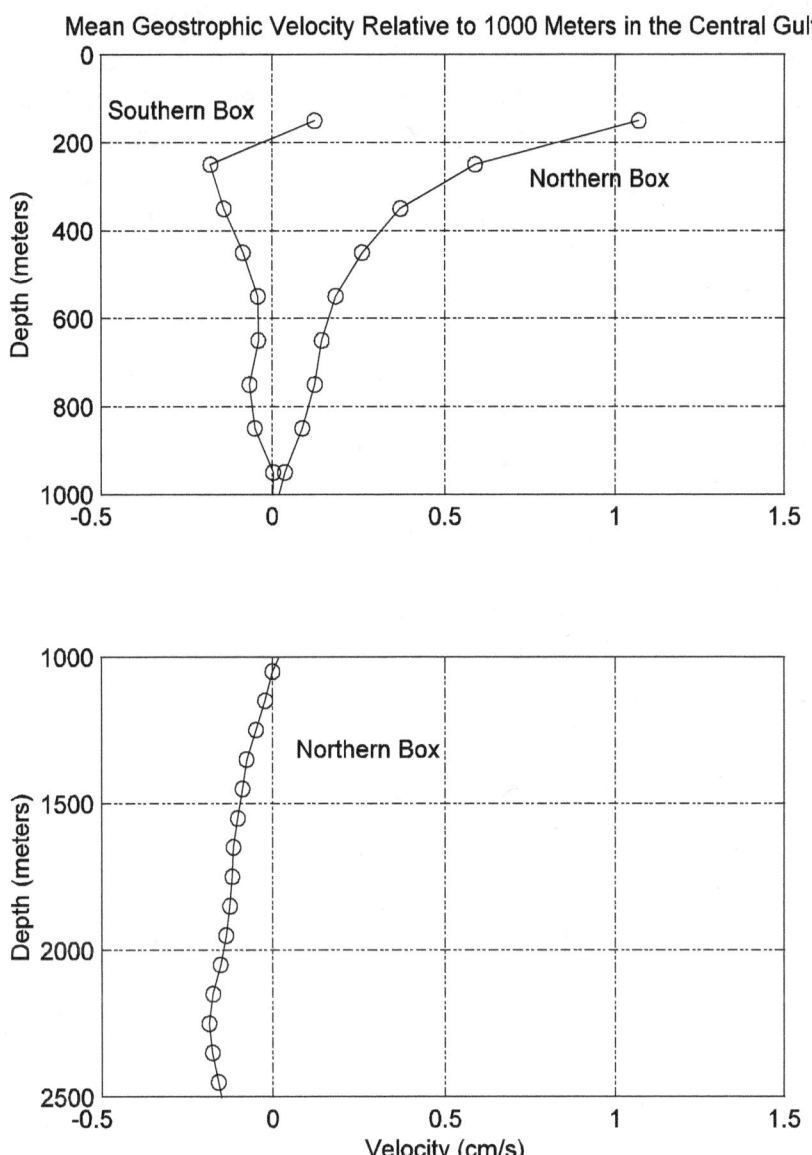

Figure 3.5. Mean E-W speeds, relative to 1,000 db, computed from the
temperature signal in the central Gulf. The result is shown for the
deeper section only for the northern half, where the signal-to-noise
ratio allows a significant result.

17

few tenths of a cm s^{-1}. This value seems almost ridiculously small, but we note that, first, it *is* to the west, consistent with theoretical expectations. Second, the shear profile at depth is monotonic almost to the bottom. (We would not bet heavily on the small bend at the bottom.) The actual velocity signal of the expected flow, if it is concentrated in a fairly narrow region near the boundary, will of course not be sampled closely in these average data. Thus high speeds would be almost impossible to see by this calculation, although we should certainly get the sign right. These factors all support the cyclonic hypothesis we have put forward.

3.1.3. Western Gulf

The averaging areas, or boxes, shown in Figure 3.1 also show areas in the western Gulf where we made calculations similar to those shown previously. We formed two pairs of regions there, north and south of 24° N: a north-western pair and a southwestern pair. Figure 3.6 shows the velocity profile from the southwestern pair. There we see speeds (relative to 1,000 m) of order 0.5 cm s^{-1}. The flow is to the south. This result, too, based on data completely independent from that of the previous sections, is consistent with the assumption of cyclonic flow. For the northwestern region, in the western Gulf, however, the region is "data poor" and the signal does not emerge above the noise.

3.1.4. Variability of the Geostrophic Shear

The geostrophic results presented in the preceding sections show our best attempts at determining *mean values*. To what extent, one wonders, is it possible to estimate the variability of the geostrophic velocity?

Figure 3.7 shows a collection of 46 station pairs from which we computed *individual velocity shear* patterns. The stations in each pair are from a single cruise. The data are from the same dataset as those in the previous section, but are treated quite differently. The reason for this additional calculation, obviously, is that we assumed (or at least hoped) that using pairs of stations from individual cruises might improve the accuracy of the individual calculations because calibration issues would be minimized.

As would be expected, the means from these calculations are essentially the same as from the previous calculations. There are many reversals in sign, but similar means emerge. In an attempt to construct the most accurate values, we have computed an absolute mean at each level from which to compute the standard deviations. Table 3.1 shows these results. In this case only, the values are

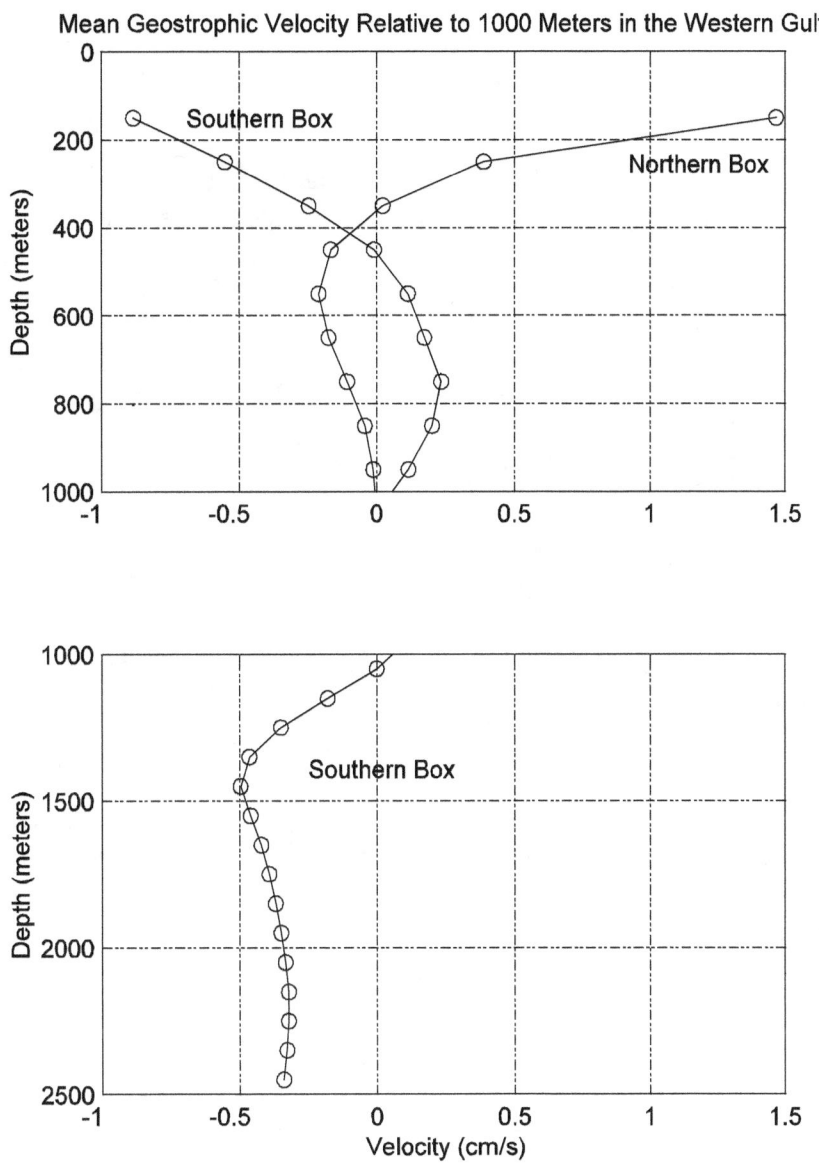

Figure 3.6. Mean N-S geostrophic speeds relative to 1,000 m in the Western Gulf of Mexico.

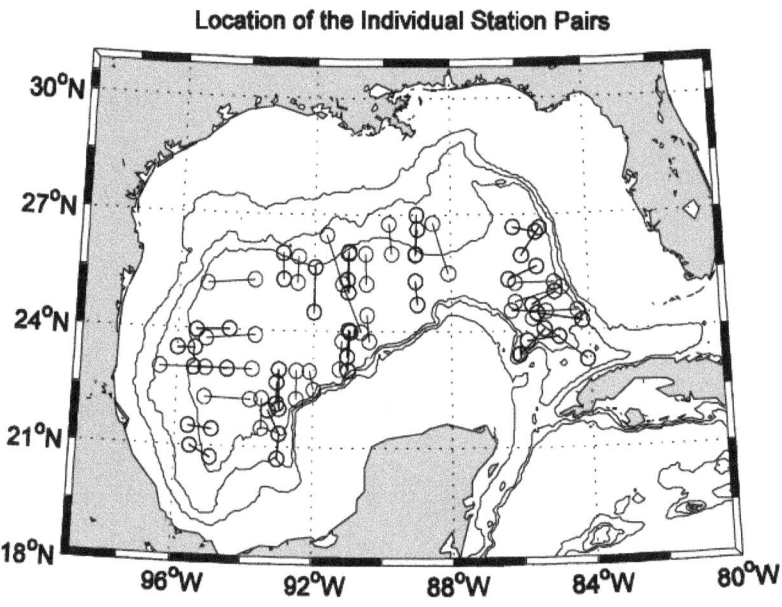

Location of the Individual Station Pairs

Figure 3.7. Locations of station pairs (from single cruises) from which geostrophic velocities were computed. Results are shown in Table 3.1 (see text).

Table 3.1

Mean Velocity Shear and Standard Deviation Relative to 2,000 db

Depth	Mean Velocity Magnitude cm/sec	Standard Deviation of Velocity
100	16.7	15.0
500	5.7	5.1
1,000	2.1	2.1
1,500	0.5	0.5

(These values were calculated by finding the absolute magnitude of all the individual station pairs and taking the mean and standard deviations.)

computed relative to 2,000 m to allow consistent comparisons at varying depths. The standard deviations of the values are similar to the speeds themselves, in part because the means are so near zero. Because these are determined from 46 individual calculations, the standard errors of the mean would be reduced by ~6.7 (i.e., $\sqrt{45}$), suggesting that the mean values are indeed significantly different from zero.

There is an important point that perhaps should be emphasized. The mean speeds are small, but the individual velocity values are strong. The fact that the individual velocity values are so large (i.e., the variance is large), we suspect, is why the signal-to-noise-ratio is so small.

3.2. Resolving the Reference-Level Issue: Observations of Deep Flow

3.2.1. Observations from Deep Current-Meter Moorings

Long-term current-meter moorings that are well suited to provide a check on absolute deep velocities are scarce. We have found four sets of current-meter mooring data that are appropriate as a reference for these geostrophic calculations; two older arrays in the eastern Gulf and two recent ones in the northern Gulf. They are summarized in Table 3.2. We deal first with the data farthest south, along the Florida escarpment, taken in an MMS-sponsored program in the early 1980s (Hamilton, 1990).

Figure 3.8 shows the locations of Moorings A and G; plots of the north-south (along-isobath) velocity from Mooring A are in Figure 3.9. Figure 3.10 shows the mean speeds as a function of depth.

The variability is similar at the other mooring, and the mean speeds at depth are also to the north, but the values are only barely greater than zero. That mooring, however, is farther away from the steeply-sloping face of the West Florida Escarpment.

The spectrum of the N-S velocity component at the deepest instrument shows that the energy peaks at periods of 20-30 days. (This frequency band is typical of topographic Rossby waves and will be found at other moorings as discussed later.) There are ~500 days of total record at the lower instrument, capturing ~20 "periods." Because the correlation coefficient falls to zero at one fourth of a period for a narrow-band signal, we estimate that there are approximately 80 independent observations. This conclusion leads to an estimated uncertainty (standard error of the mean) of ~0.5 cm s^{-1}. Thus we conclude that the mean value at 1600 m (Figure 3.10) of ~4 cm s^{-1} (to the north) is significantly different from zero by 8 times (!) the standard error of the mean. (Many probability tables do not show results for values greater than 4 times the standard deviation; one's assumptions about the shape of the distribution become crucial.)

Perhaps we should emphasize the main point here: the observed mean speed over nearly 3 years is several cm s^{-1} to the north and significantly different from zero *during this time interval*. However, considering the large variability of such signals on decadal time scales, we would not assume that this mean value or error estimate is valid for all time.

Table 3.2

Observations of Deep Currents Near the Edges of the Gulf of Mexico

Agency	Method	Location	Depths (m)	Dates
NOAA (Molinari)	C-M	W. Fla. Escarp, 27.5°N, 85.5°W	950	6/78-5/79
SAIC	C-M	W. Fla. Escarp., 25.6°N, 84.6°W	1,100, 1,600	1/83-1/86
NOPP	Deep Floats	Western Gulf	~900	3/98-8/02
Ensenada Group	C-M	Yucatan Channel	Full Water Column	9/99-5/01
GULL (Szabo)	C-M	Northern Gulf, 27°N 89°W-92°W	1,500-3,300	9/00-11/01
SAIC	C-M	Northern Gulf, ~90°W	32-2,164	8/99-9/01

It seems plausible, therefore, that our choice of 1,000 m as a reference level is an effective choice for the purpose at hand. Our estimated mean speed, relative to 1,000 m, was found to be ~ 1.1 cm/sec (Figure 3.3). To this we may add ~ 3 cm s^{-1} (Figure 3.10), suggesting a deep cyclonic speed in the eastern Gulf of order 3-4 cm s^{-1}. Since there probably is not a single level of "no motion" in the Gulf, 1,000 m is used, merely to be able to make comparisons between the geostrophic shear profiles; the current meter moorings suggest that this choice is eminently reasonable.

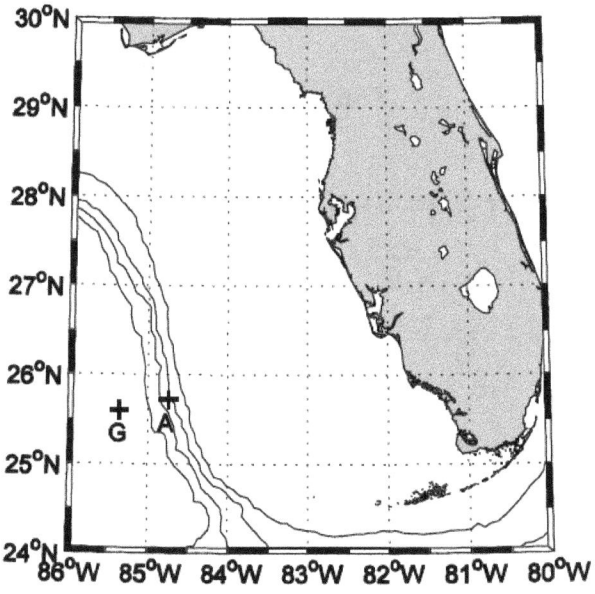

Figure 3.8. Locations of current meter Moorings A and G.

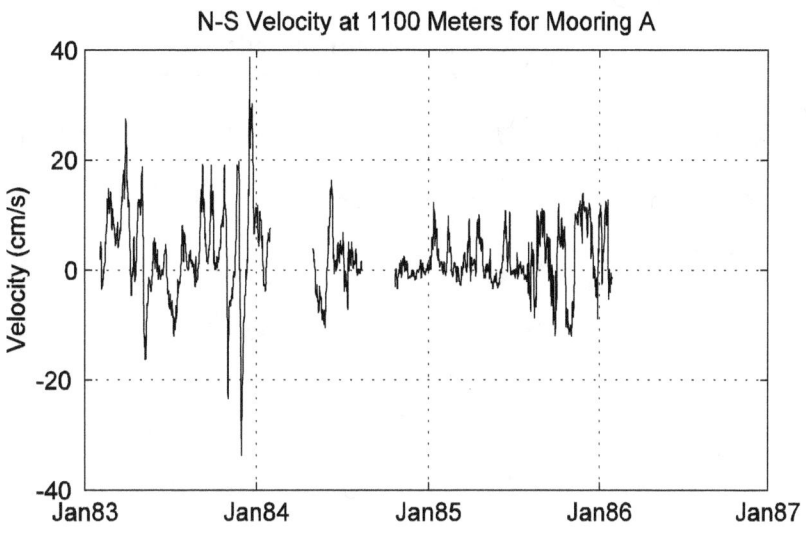

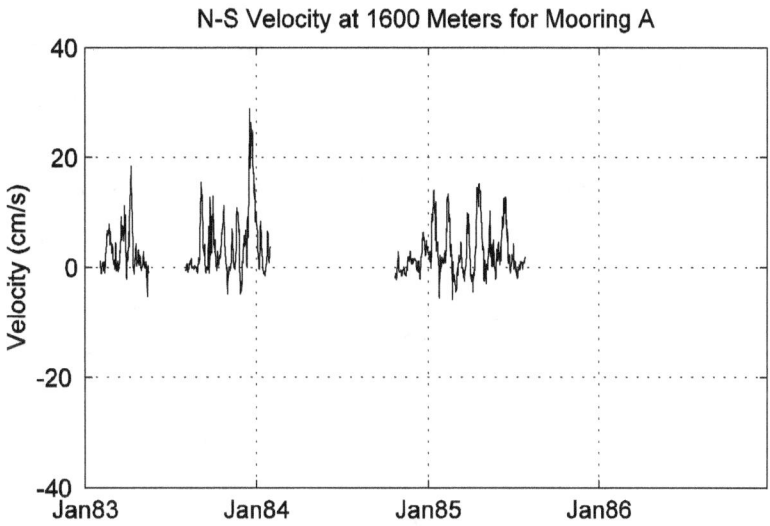

Figure 3.9. Velocity records at the deepest instruments on Mooring A (the location of Mooring A is shown in Figure 3.8).

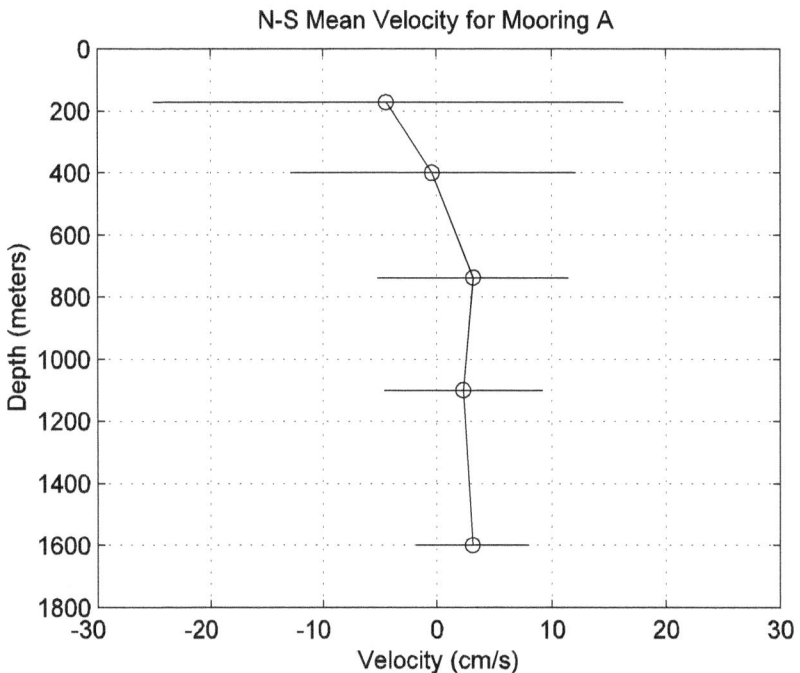

Figure 3.10. Mean velocity profile for speeds at Mooring A.

We also explored the possible coherence between temperature and velocity at these two moorings. If cold bursts of incoming deep water from the Caribbean Sea retain their temperature deficit this far into the Gulf, it would be an interesting finding. Unfortunately, the temperature signals were barely resolved at each instrument, and there was no clear coherence between velocity and temperature. At depths near 1,600 m, the deepest instrument at Mooring A, the temperature difference between the Caribbean and Gulf water is very small, so lack of coherence there is not surprising. Near sill depth (2,000 m), the Caribbean is roughly 0.1°C cooler. However, at mooring G the nearest instrument was at ~2,360 m; temperature record was composed largely of "background temperature," with occasional departures of a few hundredths of a degree. It seems likely that the instrument was deeper than the incoming bursts of cooler water. Because there were so many "background temperature" data points, which appear as "zero" in a calculation of the spectrum, we considered the calculations of cross-spectral coherence to be of questionable validity.

It is instructive to estimate the transports associated with these deep flows. At Mooring A, the inshore mooring, the mean nearly-barotropic N-S velocity is ~3 cm/sec, over a depth span of at least 1,000 m and possibly twice that. If we take the horizontal extent to be only 75 km (the distance to Mooring G, farther offshore) the mean transport is thus estimated to be ~3 to 6 Sv. This mean value applies to a narrow boundary current.
For the stronger bursts of flow, however, the speeds are easily 25 cm/sec at Mooring G, and clearly are barotropic to ~3,200 m. It is hard to escape the conclusion that the transports in these bursts (to the north) are much larger than our estimate for the boundary flow. The estimated transports for brief periods in the deeper layers in Yucatan (see, for example, Bunge et al. 2002) from the recent moorings there are consistent with these surprisingly large values.

Additional evidence for northerly flow along the steep slopes off west Florida, from deep long-term moorings, is found in the work of Molinari and Mayer (1980). They measured the flow at ~1,000 m offshore of Tampa, FL (near 27.5°N; see Figure 3.8 above). They show (their Figure 33) that at the uppermost mooring (at 150 m) there was almost no net along-isobath flow for the whole year (June 1978 to May 1979). At the deepest mooring (950 m, 100 m above the bottom) there was flow to the north, along the isobaths, of the order of 5 cm s^{-1} in 9 out of 11 months. In the other two months (November and December) the flow was essentially in the noise level. The mean flow at the deepest mooring over the full record was

~3.3 cm/sec to the northwest, the orientation of the local isobaths. Thus their measurements, although taken in different years, are remarkably consistent with the results of the SAIC moorings shown in Figure 3.10.

Several current-meter mooring arrays have been installed in the north-central Gulf in recent years. One set of moorings that is relevant to our present discussion was installed by Fugro GEOS in their GULL program. Their array was composed of nineteen moorings on which instruments were placed approximately 100 and 300 m from the bottom, in water depths of ~ 1,600 m to ~3,400 m. Several groups of moorings were located between 89°W and 91°W, from late August 2000 through November 2001. The major difference between the results from these moorings and the data from the West Florida Escarpment is that the flow near steep bottom topography in the northern Gulf near 90° W (i.e., the Sigsbee Escarpment) is somewhat more energetic; the speeds are greater than those shown in Figure 3.9. With these moorings it is possible to see that, in the mean, the deeper flow is strong and toward the west, again consistent with the cyclonic deep flow hypothesis. This dataset remains proprietary at the time of this writing.

The final set of moorings that is relevant to our discussion has been reported recently by Hamilton and Lugo-Fernandez (2001). There were 4 moorings in an array near 27°N, 90°W, measuring flow especially near the bottom (as well as full water column) at depths near 2,000 m.

The mean speeds near the bottom, at 2,000 m, ranged from ~2 to 4.2 cm/sec, all to the west (along the local topography). The highest speeds were seen at mooring I2; this mooring is near the center of the array and near the steepest bottom slopes. At this mooring, which had a 2-year long record, the mean speed at ~11 m above the bottom was 4.2 cm/s, with a standard deviation of 16.75 cm/sec. The TRW energy has a broad peak at ~ 20 days. (Recall that, for relatively narrow-band signals, there are essentially 4 observations per cycle.) For a two-year record the data length suggests a standard error of the mean of ~1.3 cm/sec. Thus the mean speed is more than 3 times the standard error, even in a situation with large variance. This is indeed significant, as were the results from the other mooring areas. The deep mean speeds at all 4 moorings were to the west, so if they were grouped, the significance level would be even higher.

3.2.2. Observations from Deep Drifting Floats

The best data set we have found that covers a broad region of the Gulf is composed of velocities from an experiment using PALACE (Profiling Autonomous LAgrangian Circulation Experiment) floats. These are a profiling version of the original ALACE floats (Davis, et al., 1991; see also the web site of the manufacturer, http://www.webbresearch.com). The National Ocean Partnership Program (NOPP) sponsored this experiment in the Gulf. Approximately four dozen floats were tracked from 1998-2002. A potentially serious problem is that the floats are at the surface for several hours to transmit data. The surface velocities are usually much greater than those at depth. If we were to assume that all the motion takes place at depth, there could be serious contamination of results by surface drift. But navigation fixes at the surface allow the surface drift to be estimated so that the deep float velocities can be corrected for surface motion. We are greatly indebted to our colleagues Georges Weatherly and Nicolas Wienders for allowing us to use their prepublication results (Wienders et al., 2002; Weatherly and Wienders, 2003).

Figure 3.11 shows the computed means and variance ellipses after the corrections have been applied. The mean velocity vectors for this figure were obtained by averaging all the float velocities in 0.5° bins. For these results, only bins with more than 5 float values were used (an admittedly arbitrary choice). While the mean values are small, there is a robust tendency toward a cyclonic pattern at 900 m. While some regions are sampled poorly (and some not at all), the tendency for cyclonic flow, just above 1,000 m, is evident. (In case it is "hard to see," the small vectors have arrowheads pointing in the direction of mean flow.)
The major purpose here is not, strictly speaking, to determine exactly the velocity at 1,000 m, but to determine the validity of our choice of 1,000 m as an adequate reference level for the geostrophic calculations. Careful examination of Figure 3.11 shows that the flow near the edges of the basin has become cyclonic, albeit weakly, at 900 m. Our calculations suggest, of course, that the speeds increase, by roughly ~1 to 2 cm/sec, down to ~2,000 m (see Table 2).

3.3. Path of Cold Renewal Water

At depths of 2,000 m, the Caribbean Sea is colder by ~ 0.1°C than the Gulf. The results of the Mexican mooring experiment in Yucatan (Bunge et al., 2002) show that cold Caribbean water pours in at Yucatan Channel during every Loop Current cycle. So if there is a deep cyclonic boundary flow, we expect that the temperature around the edges of the deep Gulf should be coldest near Yucatan where the "new" renewal water enters, . We would expect that the cold signal, or temperature deficit, would decay with distance "downstream" from Yucatan, as is observed in all such overflow situations (in the Mediterranean outflow, Denmark Strait overflow, etc.; see for example Girton and Sanford 2003).

Figure 3.11. Mean velocity of drifters at 900 m over the course of several years. The freely-drifting floats surfaced every 7 days; velocity values have been corrected for surface drift effects. These are averaged in ½-degree bins (courtesy of Weatherly and Wienders, 2003). Values are shown only for bins that have 5 or more observations.

To examine the possibility of such an effect, Figure 3.12 shows the potential temperature at 2,000 m, averaged in one-degree boxes around the edge, plotted as a function of distance from Yucatan. Because the path is irregular, the x-axis is only very roughly a measure of the distance from the source of cold water entering at Yucatan. The individual mean data values are shown, with a smoothed curve through the scattered data points. The increase in temperature with distance from Yucatan is strikingly clear. The sharpest gradient is nearest the entrance at Yucatan, which is consistent with strong initial mixing. Apart from this strong gradient in the first half-dozen data points, a linear fit through the other data would be adequate. The total increase in temperature is ~0.07°C, which is surprisingly consistent with the net difference in temperature between the two basins. This effect could be interpreted as an indication of the cyclonic boundary flow. However, it is entirely possible that the supply of cold water at Yucatan is one possible mechanism for *causing* the boundary flow, in a manner similar to that of the Deep Western Boundary Current along the U.S. east coast. The historical data set is adequate at 2,000 m to see the changes in Figure 3.12, but at greater depths the sampling is strongly concentrated near 2,500 m and 3,000 m. The mean (potential) temperature in the Gulf continues to decrease only by ~ 0.02°C between 2,000 m and 3,000 m. A better understanding of the mechanisms and details of the deep-water renewal remains for future work.

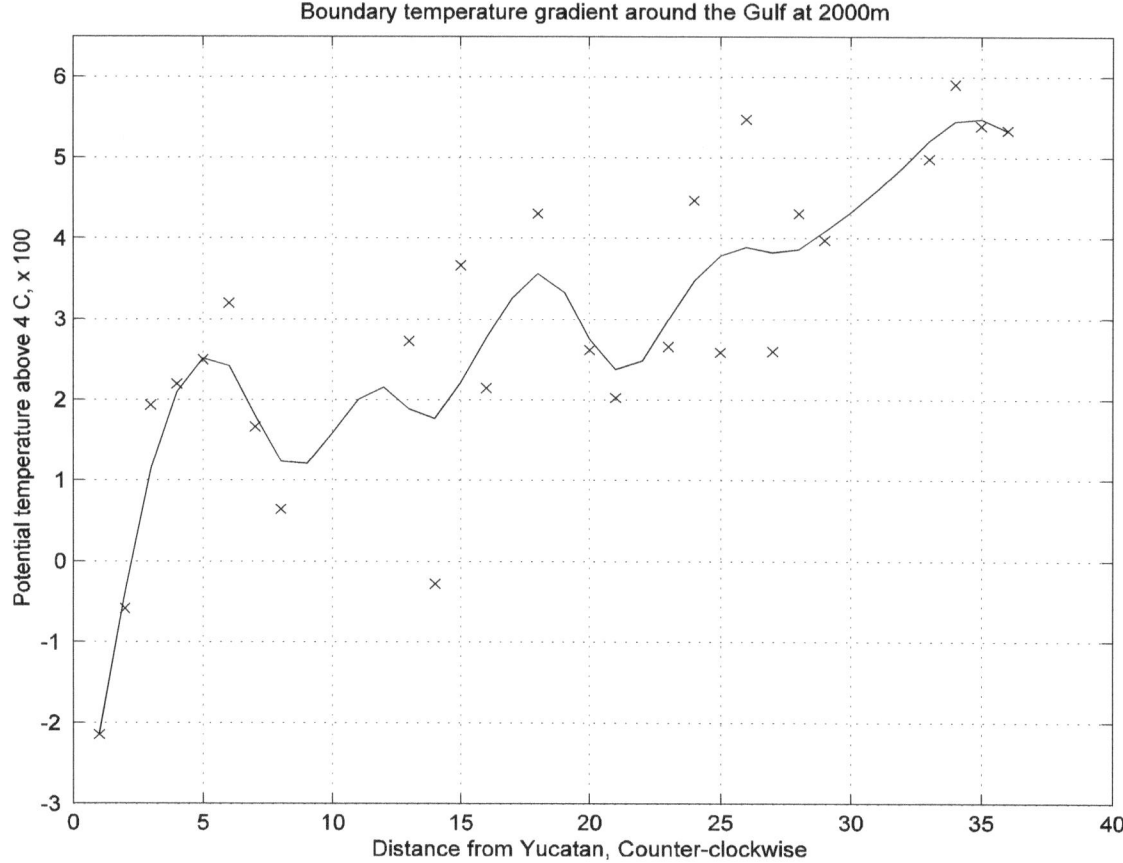

Figure 3.12. Time-mean potential temperature around the edge of the Gulf of Mexico at 2,000 m, averaged in one-degree boxes, plotted as a function of distance from the sill in Yucatan Channel. The x-axis is roughly a measure of distance. The individual mean data points are shown (x); if a one-degree box had no data, linear interpolation was used for this figure, and the curve connecting the points was smoothed slightly. Except for the data points nearest Yucatan, a least-squares straight-line fit would probably be adequate. Note that the potential temperature values have had 4.0 subtracted from them.

For completeness, Figure 3.13 shows the details of the mean potential temperature distribution, averaged in one-degree boxes, at 2,000 m. In each one-degree box, the upper number shows the number of samples from the NODC data base. The lowest figure is the standard error of the mean in that box. From each mean temperature, the value 4.00 has been subtracted; thus a value of "7.3" implies a true potential temperature of 4.073° C. (Some people use the term "anomalies" for such values.) The data in Figure 3.12 are of course completely consistent with this figure, as they are from the same data base. Although this figure represents the entire existing historical data base from U.S. ships, we note that there remain 14 one-degree boxes with no data (including boxes with partial areas deeper than 2,000 m).

Our calculations of density in the deep water were based on a mean t,S curve. Figure 3.14 presents the over-all potential temperature-salinity properties of the deep Gulf. Salinity is plotted as a function of potential temperature for a collection of all deep U.S. hydro stations on file at NODC. We show only data colder than 6.0 C, an isotherm that lies well above 1,000 m. The choice of U.S. data only was in an attempt to reduce the uncertainties in salinity calibrations. The individual data points show a series of mean potential temperature and salinity points, together with the standard deviation in salinity. This plot shows the results after a "pruning" to remove points that fell outside 3 standard deviations.

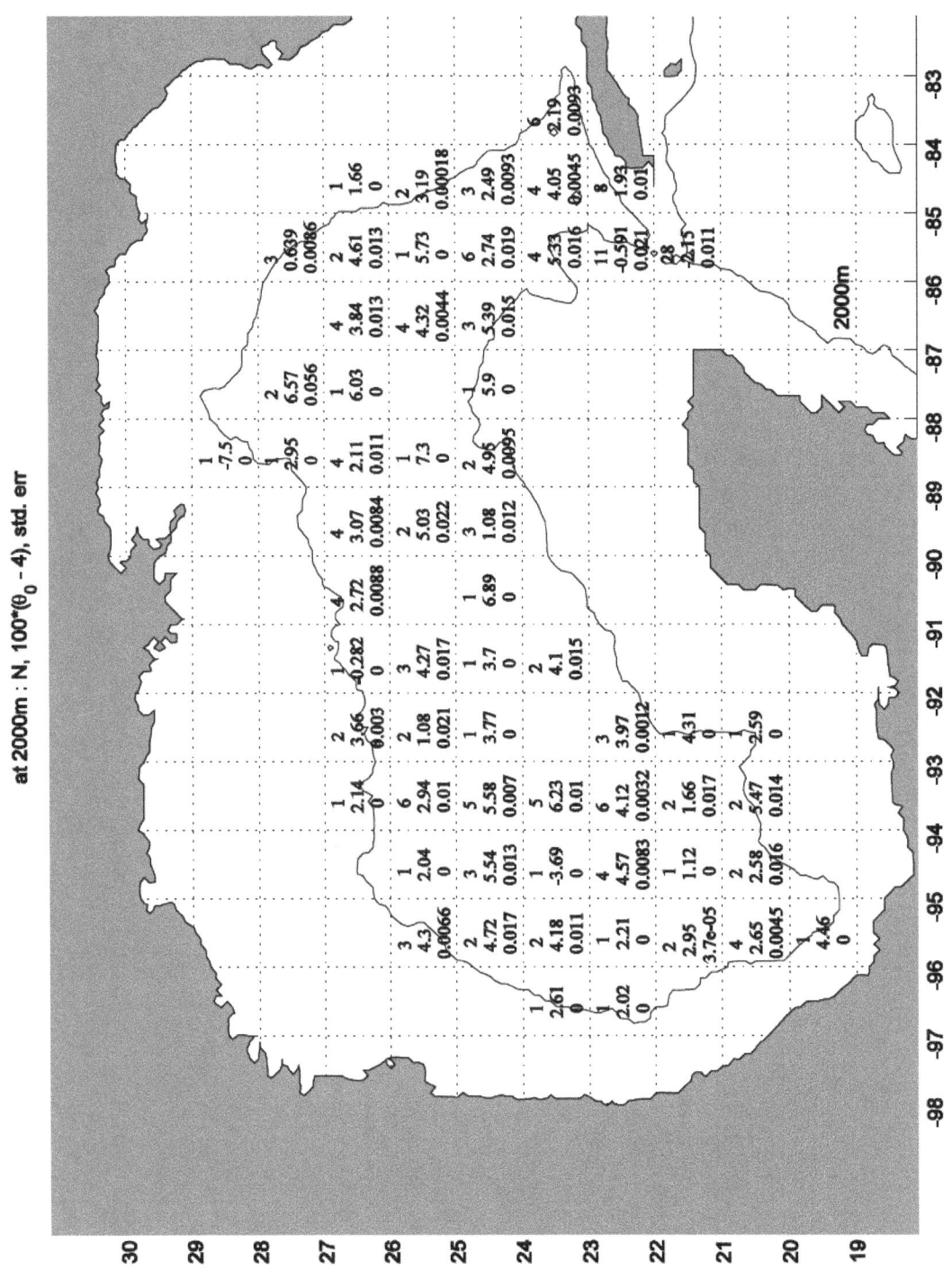

Figure 3.13. Mean temperature at 2,000 m. In each box all available U.S. data were averaged. The number of samples, the mean potential temperature and standard error are shown. From each mean temperature, 4.00°C has been subtracted; thus a value of 7.3 implies a true temperature of 4.073°C.

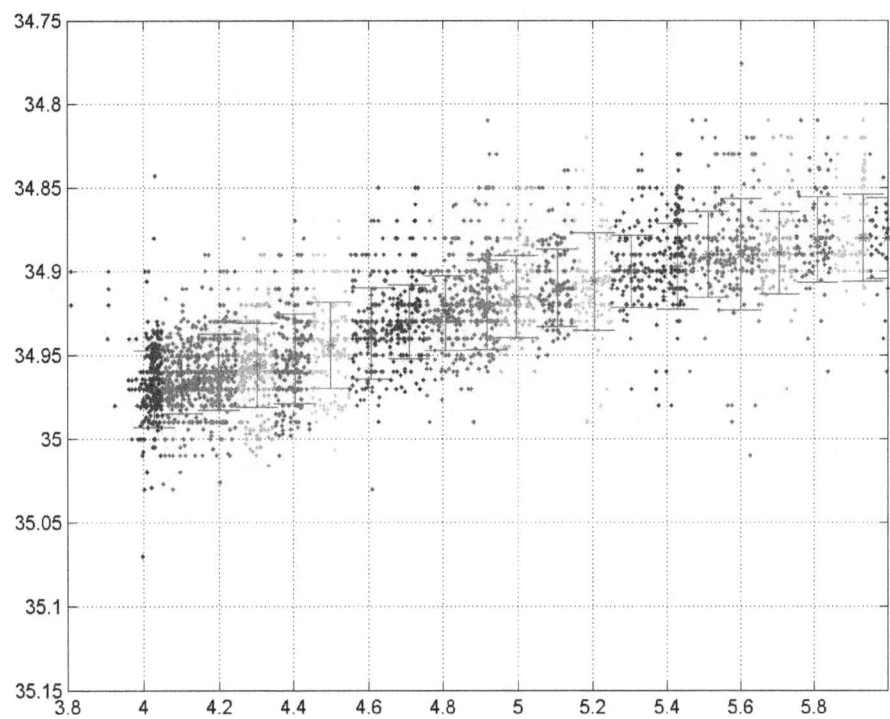

Figure 3.14. Potential temperature-salinity properties of the deep Gulf. Salinity
(vertical axis) is plotted as a function of potential temperature for all
deep U.S. hydro stations on file at NODC for data colder than 6.0° C.
The individual data points (red dots and bars) show a series of mean
potential temperature and salinity points and the standard deviation in
salinity. This plot shows the results after a "pruning" to remove
points that fell outside 3 standard deviations.

4. RESULTS FROM NUMERICAL MODELING: STUDIES USING THE PRINCETON MODEL

4.1. Description of the Princeton Ocean Model

The numerical model is based on the sigma-coordinate (or terrain-following) Princeton Ocean Model (POM) (Blumberg and Mellor, 1987). For a recent description, please see the web page for this model located at: http://www.aos.princeton.edu/WWWPUBLIC/htdocs.pom. The northwest Atlantic Ocean implementation of the model, known as the Princeton Regional Ocean Forecast System (PROFS), is described in detail by Oey and Lee (2002; http://www.aos.princeton.edu/WWWPUBLIC/PROFS) and by Ezer et al. (2003). The model uses 25 layers in the vertical, with finer resolution near the surface and near the bottom. A curvilinear, orthogonal, horizontal grid is used with resolution that varies from ~5 km in the northern Gulf of Mexico to ~10 k in the Yucatan Channel and ~20 km in the open subtropical Atlantic. The model domain, 55° W to 98° W and 5° N to 50° N, includes the Gulf Stream, the Gulf of Mexico and the Caribbean Sea. Across the eastern boundary, at 55° W, constant inflow and outflow transports are specified to account for the large-scale ocean circulation component, while temperature and salinity on the boundary are based on the monthly climatology. The 6-hourly ECMWF winds are used to force the model, as are surface salt and heat fluxes and river runoff. Data assimilation is sometimes included in this model system (Wang et al., 2003), but the analyses done in this project are for runs without data assimilation, so as to account only for model dynamics without data-based corrections.

Oey et al. (2003a) conducted studies to evaluate the effect of the open boundary conditions and the "local versus remote forcing" effects on the variability of the Caribbean Sea and the Gulf of Mexico. Experiments with nested grids with doubling the resolution were done as well, but they are reported elsewhere by Oey and his group. Most of the main circulation features of the mean flows remain the same in the case of higher resolution models, though the mesoscale variability is larger and closer to the observed variability. In addition to their material covered in this report, this work has been widely summarized in the published literature. See, for example, Oey and Lee (2002); Oey et al. (2003b); Ezer et al. (2002, 2003); and Wang et al. (2003).

4.2. General Circulation in the Gulf of Mexico and Comparisons Between POM and MICOM

The circulation in the Gulf of Mexico in this model shows a complicated structure with several semi-permanent gyres. Figures 4.1– 4.5 show the 5-year mean trajectories at 400 m, 500 m, 1,500 m, 2,000 m and 2,500 m, respectively. These are trajectories of particles launched at every second model grid point and propagated by the (constant) mean flow for a period of 20 days. The scale vector (in cm/s) represents the distance that a particle with that mean speed would have traveled during this period. These plots can be compared with velocity plots at similar depths from the MICOM model in Section 5 of this report. These semi-permanent gyres are affected by the propagating Loop Current eddies (i.e., averaging the effect of several eddies) and by topographical features. Some gyres are quite similar to those found in the MICOM simulations, but some are different, as would be expected. Both models show the Loop Current quite clearly, of course. The POM and the MICOM indicate an anticyclonic gyre in the western Gulf and a cyclonic gyre in Campeche Bay, in the southwest corner. These are robust features and well known.

At depths below ~1,500 m, however, the deep circulation in POM is characterized by a strong boundary-current-like cyclonic circulation, hugging the slopes, consistent with the theory and observational results put forward in Section III of this report, whereas in MICOM a weak anticyclonic circulation is found at this depth along the boundary. In higher resolution POM calculations this boundary current has larger variability and weaker mean, but its main direction remains cyclonic. At 2,500 m (2,000 m in MICOM) both models indicate a cyclonic gyre around 92°-94°W and 24°N. Figures 4.3- 4.5 show that the flow near the boundaries is cyclonic—as found in Section III and here—but the interior flow is much more complex than a mere single gyre.

Vertical sections of the flow show us another view of the model results. Figure 4.6 shows a N-S section at 90° W in the central Gulf. There is a good bit of detail in the interior, but the point of the figure here is to show the strong flows near the boundaries. The flow on the steep slopes along the coast of Mexico is striking. The horizontal maps of Figures 4.1-4.5 show some of the same information of course, but in this presentation it shows up differently. So far as we are aware there are no direct observations of this flow along the Mexican continental rise.

AVR. VEL.   400M

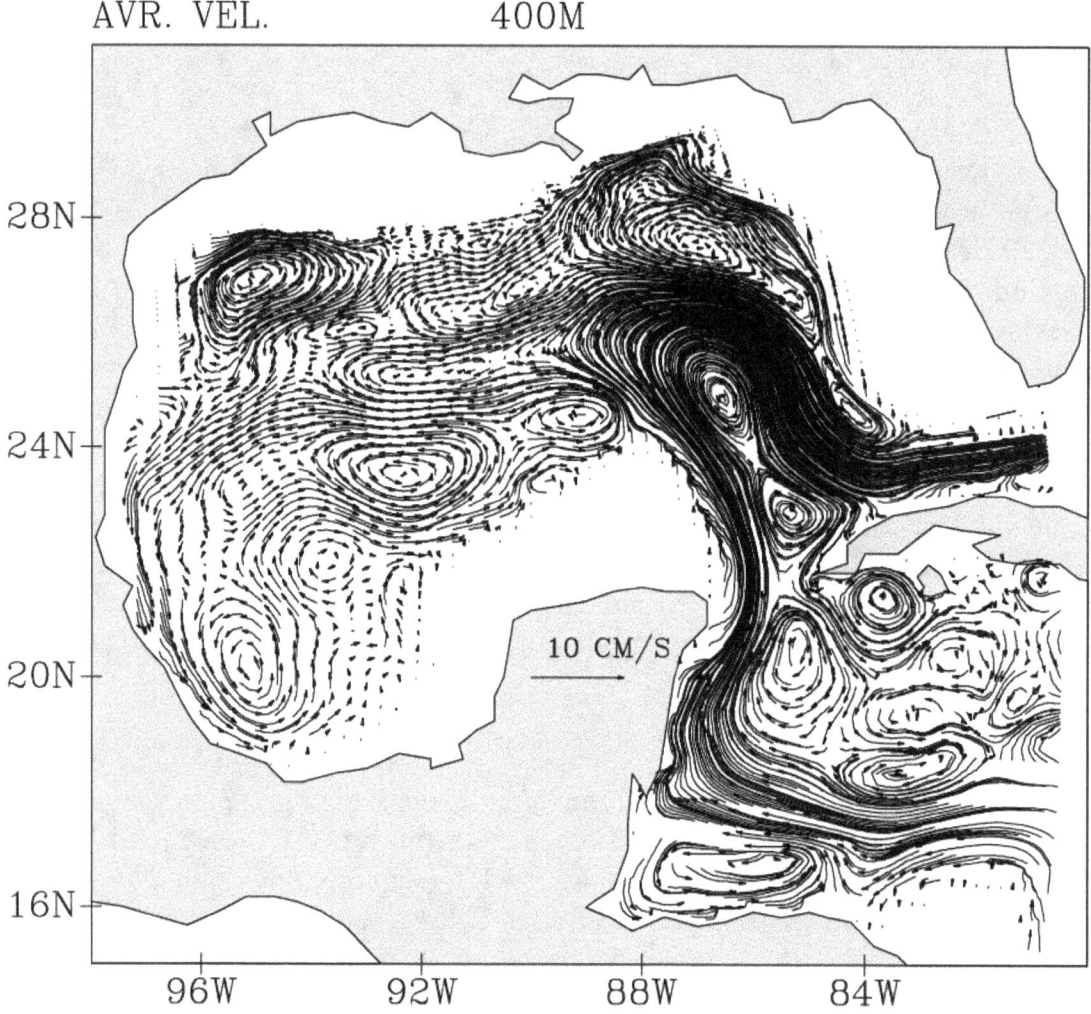

Figure 4.1. Trajectory plot based on the 5-year mean velocity at 400-m depth from
POM forced by 6-hourly ECMWF winds but without data
assimilation. These are trajectories of particles launched at every
second model grid point and propagated by the (constant) mean flow
for a period of 20 days. The scale vector (in cm/s) represents the
distance that a particle with that mean speed would have traveled
during this period.

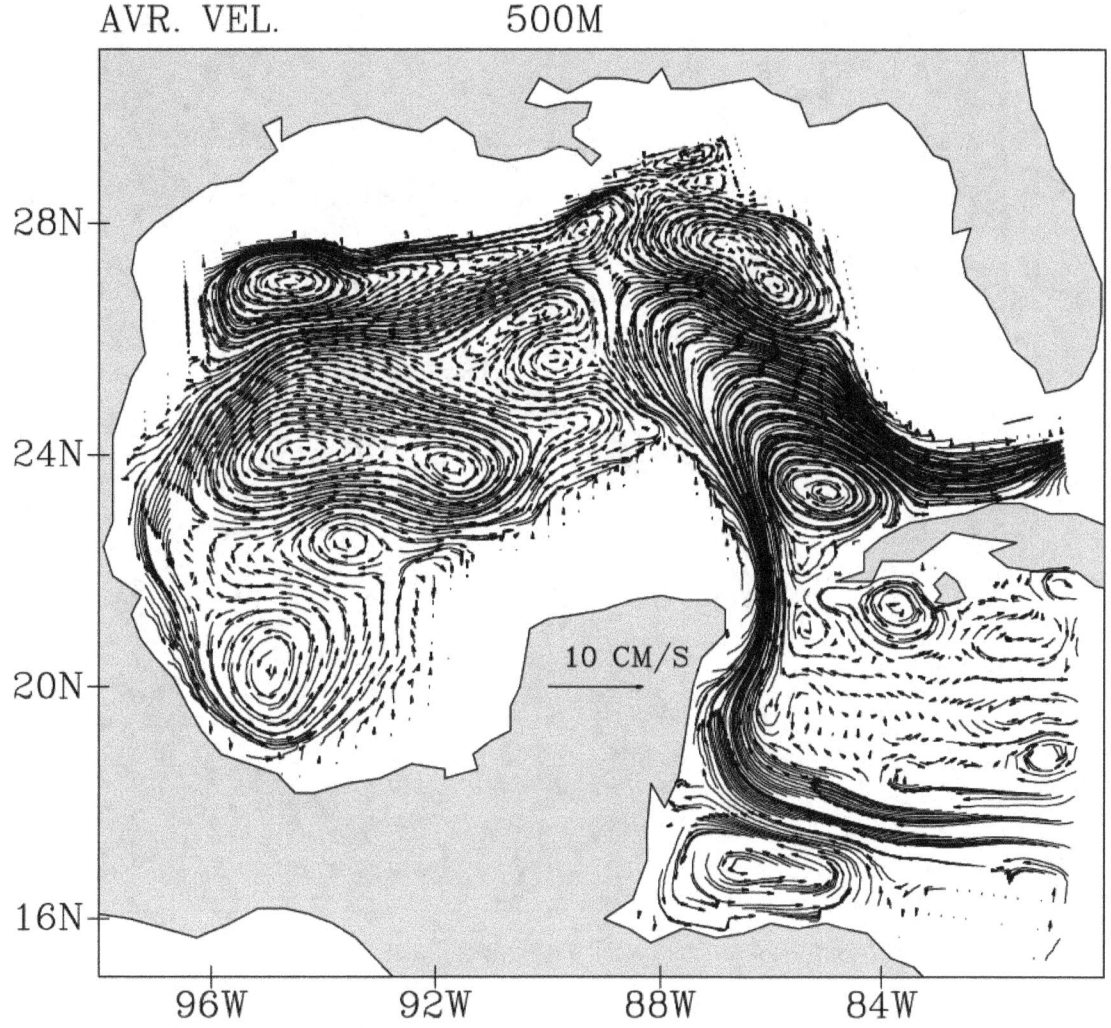

Figure 4.2. Trajectory plot based on the 5-year mean velocity at 500-m depth from POM forced by 6-hourly ECMWF winds but without data assimilation. These are trajectories of particles launched at every second model grid point and propagated by the (constant) mean flow for a period of 20 days. The scale vector (in cm/s) represents the distance that a particle with that mean speed would have traveled during this period.

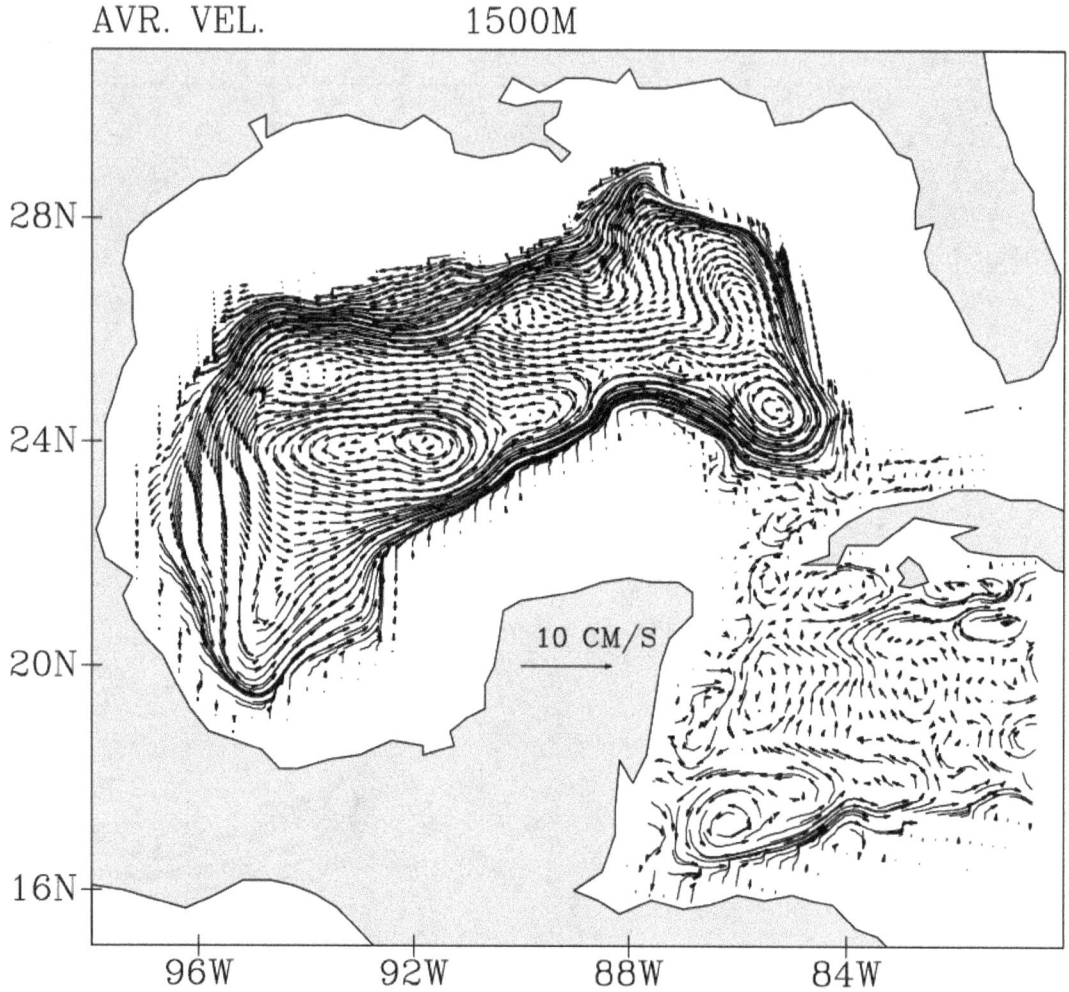

Figure 4.3. Trajectory plot based on the 5-year mean velocity at 1,500-m depth from POM forced by 6-hourly ECMWF winds but without data assimilation. These are trajectories of particles launched at every second model grid point and propagated by the (constant) mean flow for a period of 20 days. The scale vector (in cm/s) represents the distance that a particle with that mean speed would have traveled during this period.

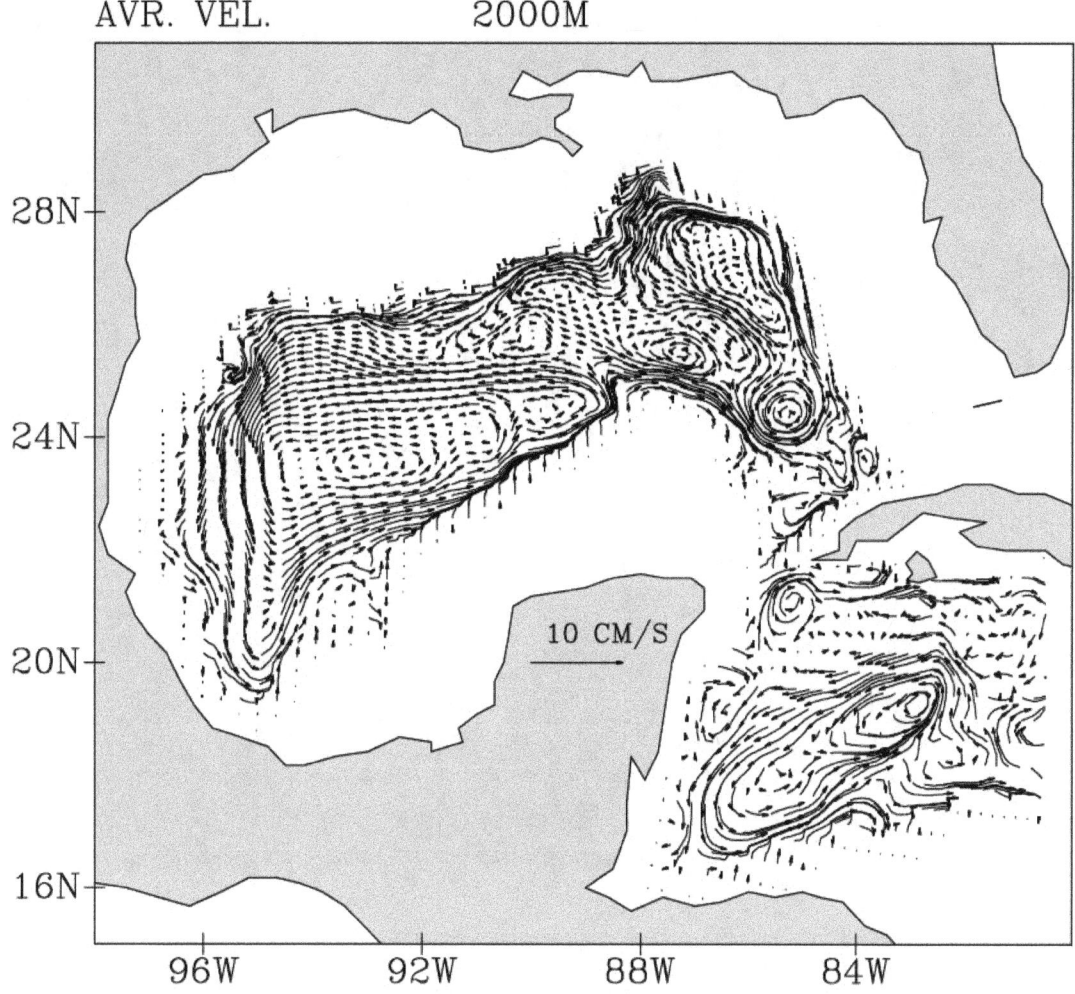

AVR. VEL.   2000M

Figure 4.4. Trajectory plot based on the 5-year mean velocity at 2,000-m depth
from POM forced by 6-hourly ECMWF winds but without data
assimilation. These are trajectories of particles launched at every
second model grid point and propagated by the (constant) mean flow
for a period of 20 days. The scale vector (in cm/s) represents the
distance that a particle with that mean speed would have traveled
during this period.

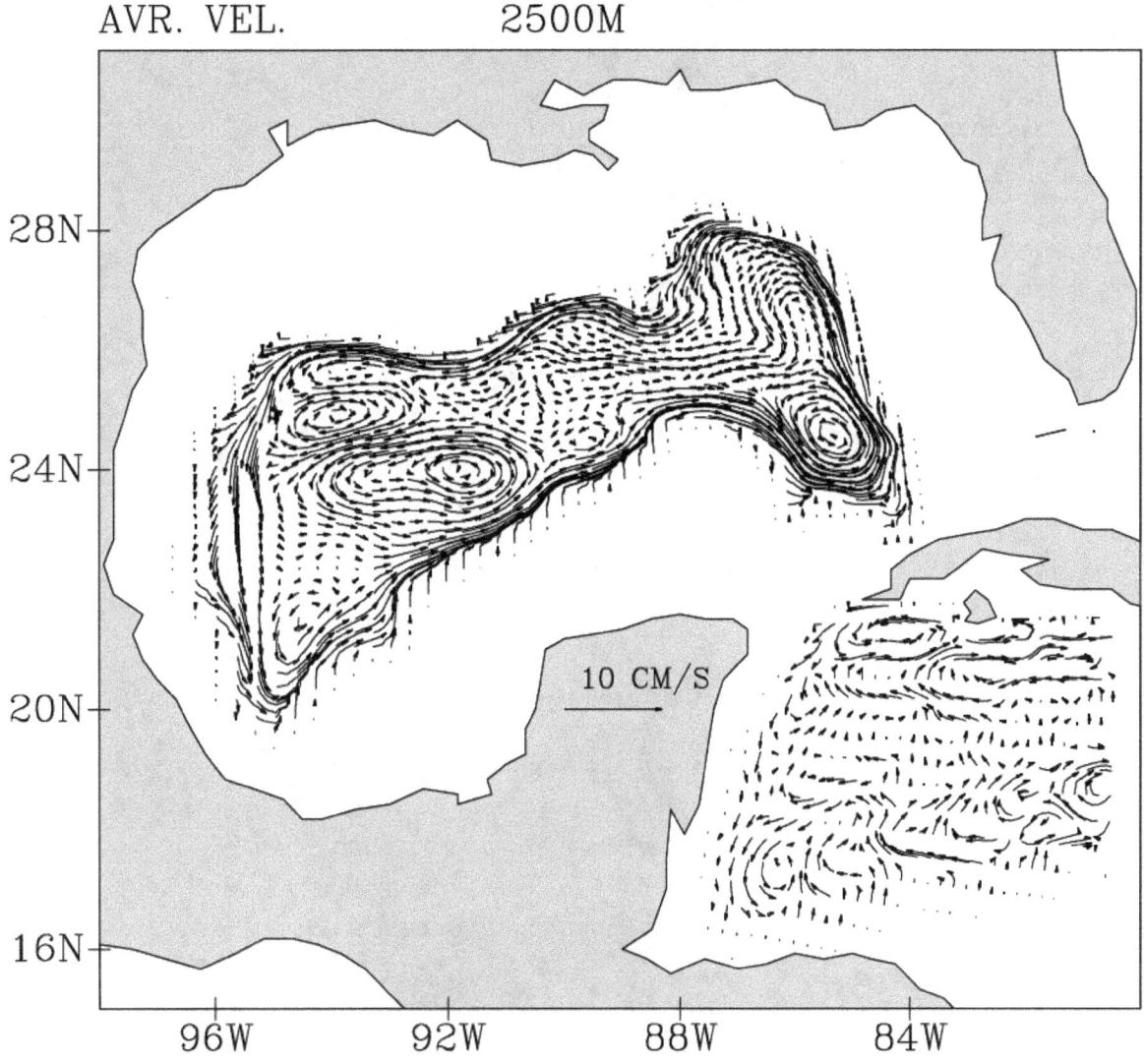

Figure 4.5. Trajectory plot based on the 5-year mean velocity at 2,500-m depth
from POM forced by 6-hourly ECMWF winds but without data
assimilation. These are trajectories of particles launched at every
second model grid point and propagated by the (constant) mean flow
for a period of 20 days. The scale vector (in cm/s) represents the
distance that a particle with that mean speed would have traveled
during this period.

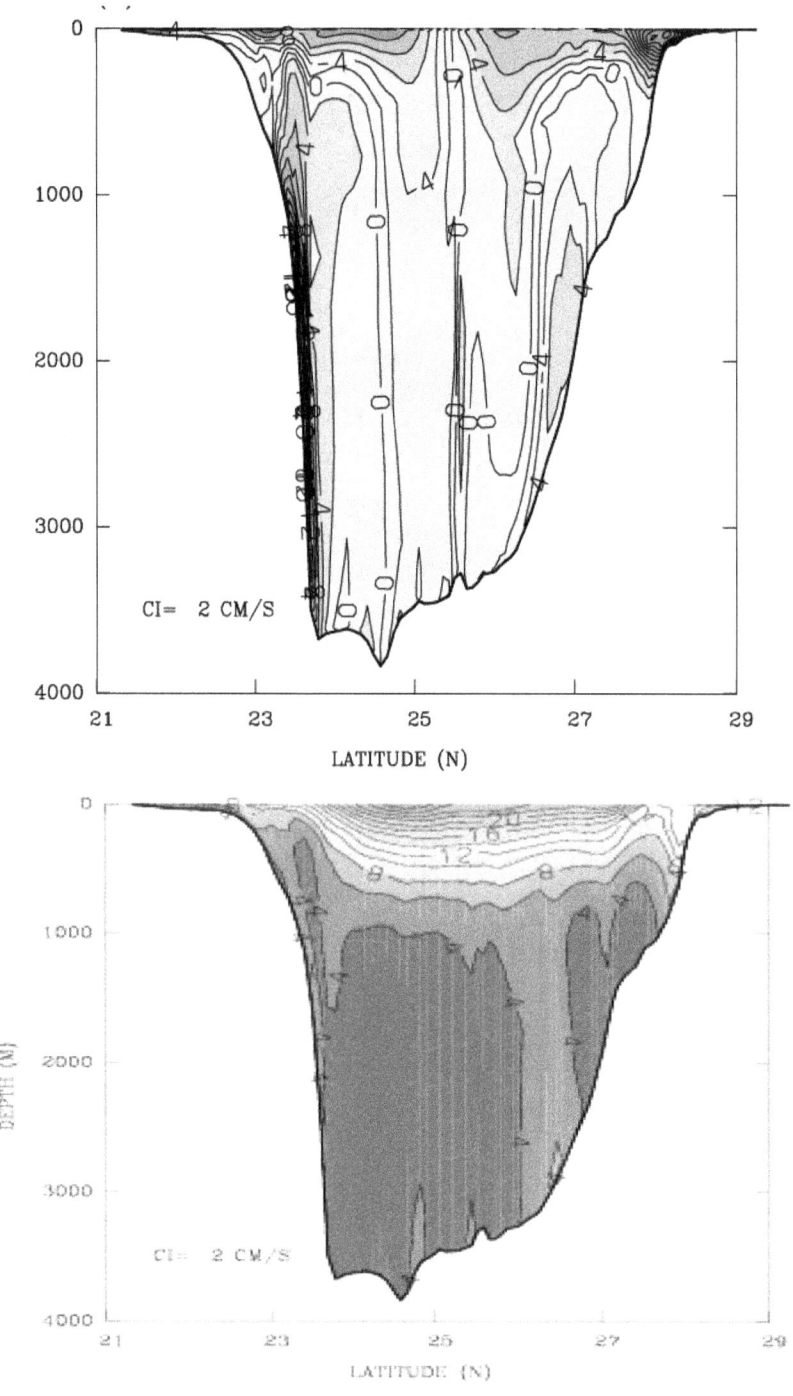

Figure 4.6.   Mean E-W (U) velocity component along a N-S section at 90° W from POM. The upper figure shows the mean speed and the lower figure shows the standard deviation.

Examining this N-S section in some detail, the model allows us to see the different phases of the flow as a large ring passes. Figure 4.7 shows four cross sections of the flow before, during, and after a ring drifts to the west. The schematic in the lower right corner of each figure shows the position of the Loop Current and the ring. The sequence is upper left to lower left, then upper right to lower right. In the third frame, as the ring is centered on the section, a "true believer" might be willing to see hints of a Taylor column of fluid being carried beneath the center of the ring. In such an interpretation the return flow to compensate for mass balance is on either side.

Another difference between the POM and MICOM models is found in the deep circulation in the eastern Gulf, under the Loop Current. Whereas a seemingly barotropic anticyclonic circulation remains in MICOM throughout the water column, a reverse, cyclonic circulation is seen in POM (as well as in Welsh's calculations using the modular version of the Bryan-Cox-Semptner, or MOM, model).

Comparisons (not shown here) of velocity and temperature cross sections at 26°N and 90°W in the two models support the above results and indicates that the MICOM flow may be more barotropic, while the POM flows are more baroclinic and more strongly affected by bottom topography, creating stronger deep boundary currents. To explain the differences between the results of the two models, one must understand the differences between the two model types. The vertical grid in MICOM follows isopycnal surfaces. Thus in the deep ocean, where stratification is very weak, the resolution can possibly be reduced. The terrain-following vertical grid in POM, on the other hand, as well as the manner in which it has been implemented here, has finer resolution and thus supports intense mixing. This is true both near the bottom, resolving the Bottom Boundary Layer (BBL), and near the surface, resolving the Surface Mixed Layer (SML). Oey and Lee (2002) have shown that the deep boundary current along the slopes of the Gulf is, to a large extent, the result of Topographic Rossby Waves (TRW) induced by fluctuations in the Loop Current and its associated eddies. Adequate resolution near the bottom is necessary to resolve the TRWs. In both models and observations, cross sections of temperature and salinity near the deep boundary current show very weak density gradients, hence the difficulty of calculating these currents from hydrographic measurements as reported in Section III above. These boundary currents are much more pronounced in observations based on floats or current meters, as one would expect. Direct comparisons of POM currents and observations are in fact quite good (e.g., Wang et al., 2003).

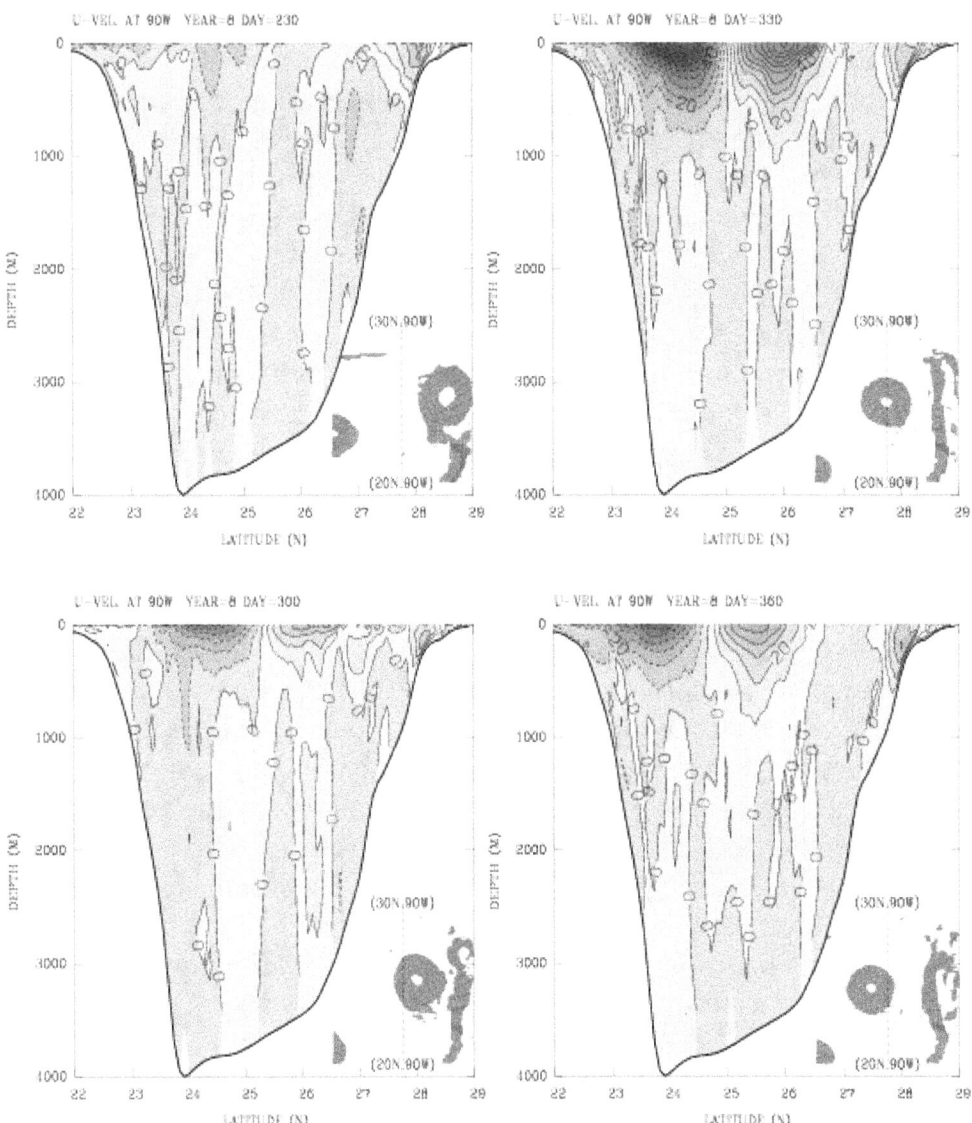

Figure 4.7. The instantaneous flow pattern along the 90° W section at four phases of a ring passage (from POM). The schematic in the lower right corner shows the positions of the ring and of the Loop Current. The sequence begins in the upper left, then to the lower left; then from the upper right to lower right.

46

4.3. Effects of Propagating Loop Current Eddies on the Deep Circulation

The Gulf is dominated by Loop Current eddy shedding events and the westward propagation of those eddies. One of the basic questions yet to be fully investigated is the effect of the eddies on the mean deep circulation. Oey and Lee (2002) have been able to demonstrate the indirect influence of eddies through generation of the TRWs. For example, as eddies propagate to the west they carry fluid with them in the upper ocean, so a return transport to the east is expected. However, the mean horizontal flow is dominated by the much stronger boundary currents and the semi-permanent gyres, so there is no clear evidence as to where this weak return transport occurs; see Figures 4.1-4.5.

To investigate this interesting question, we show (in Figure 4.8) the net transport below 800 m across 90°W (blue line). The average surface elevation across the section (green dashed line) indicates that whenever an eddy passes this section (peak in elevation) there is a peak in return transport (below 800 m) with net flow to the east. The correlation between the two curves is striking. By contrast, the net *return* deep transport, averaged over many eddies, is less than 1 Sv. In comparison with the much larger transports associated with Loop Current Rings, this small transport could easily be lost in the noise and its statistical significance would appear to be questionable. Yet we can be sure that it is a real feature of the circulation, and that the return transport must appear.

One might suspect, a priori, that there should be a Taylor column of fluid being carried along beneath the ring as it travels to the west. The fact that the model indicates increased flow back to the east when a ring passes by seems to suggest that any Taylor column effects, as mentioned in connection with Figure 4.7, are overwhelmed by other parts of the flow field. It may be that the Gulf is simply not big enough in E-W extent to allow the classic effects one might expect.

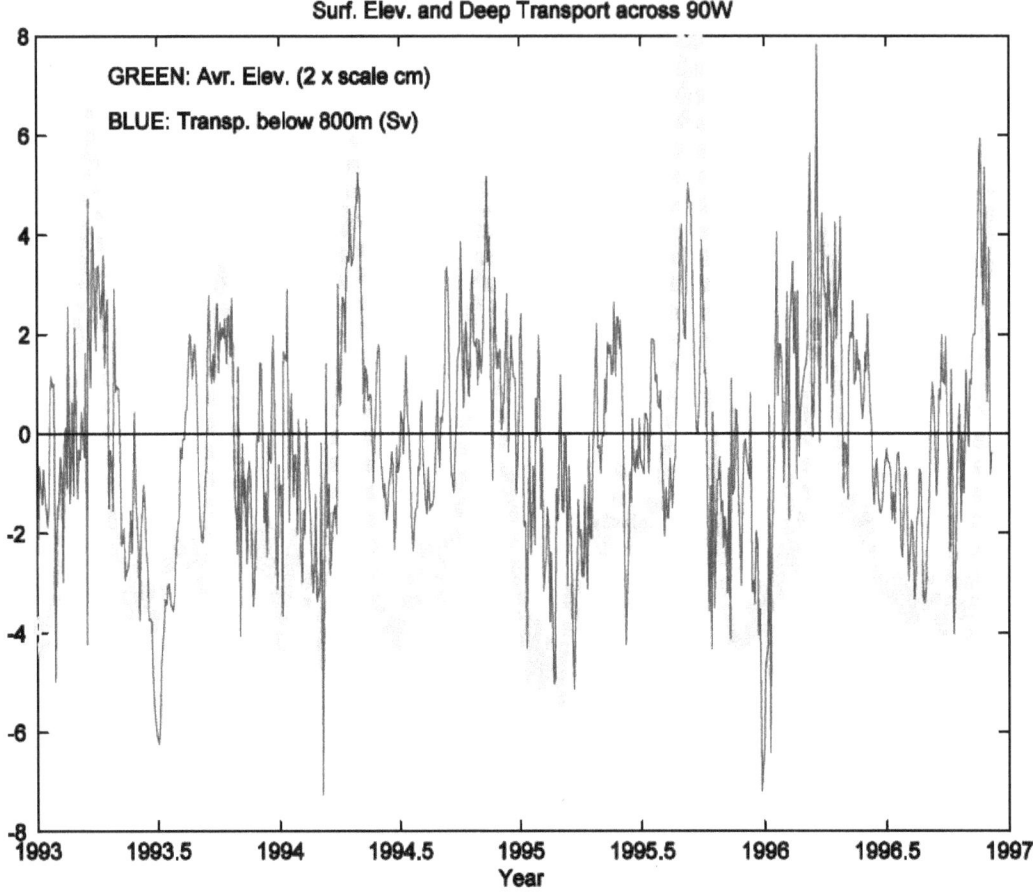

Figure 4.8. Mean surface elevation across 90°W (green dashed line) as a function of time indicates eddies (positive peaks) crossing the section. The net deep transport below 800 m across 90°W (blue solid line) indicates eastward (positive) deep transport when eddies drift westward overhead.

4.4. Variability of Flow in the Yucatan Channel and Its Relation to Variations in the Loop Current

Analysis of the model flow variability in the Yucatan Channel has three purposes. The first is to compare model results with past observations (Maul et al., 1985) as well as more recent ones (Ochoa et al., 2001; Bunge et al., 2002). The second is to understand the forcing mechanisms of the flow; the third, to determine the relation between the Yucatan Channel flow and variations of the Loop Current. For details see Ezer et al. (2002, 2003) and Oey et al. (2003b). The structure of the mean flow in the Yucatan Channel as obtained from the POM calculations seems to agree with the main features obtained from the MICOM model. Both models confirm the new finding of the existence of deep return outflows along the slopes of the Channel (Ochoa et al., 2001) and not at the center of the sill as previously thought. The net mean transport in the Yucatan Channel in our model, ~25 Sv, and the large range, ~16-32 Sv (but with no clear seasonal signal), all agree very well with the new observations of the Mexican group. EOF analysis identified the main mechanisms and forcing of the flow variability (see Ezer et al., 2003, and the description of publications supported by MMS below). For example, Figure 4.9 shows that the long-term fluctuations of the inflow from the Caribbean Sea into the Gulf (solid line) is correlated with EOF mode 2 (dashed line) of the inflow velocity across Yucatan Channel. Moreover, almost every event of eddy shedding from the Loop Current (shown by "E") is associated with a peak in the inflow transport. Such events are also associated with peaks in the return deep transport below 800 m.

Figure 4.10 is something of an unconventional plot and requires a bit of study. It shows the correlation between the changes in the deep flow (positive values in the x-axis represent southward transport below 800 m) and changes in the area of the Loop Current (positive values in the y-axis represent Loop Current growing in area). Data were taken from the passage of three eddies. We see that the deep return transport and the Loop Current extension both grow before an eddy is shed (triangles), and start decreasing afterwards (circles). Using only data points from a two-week interval before and after the ring passes, the correlation increases dramatically to 0.7. This process is consistent with the theory as proposed by Maul. et al, (1985) and recently confirmed from the new Mexican observations (Bunge et al., 2002).

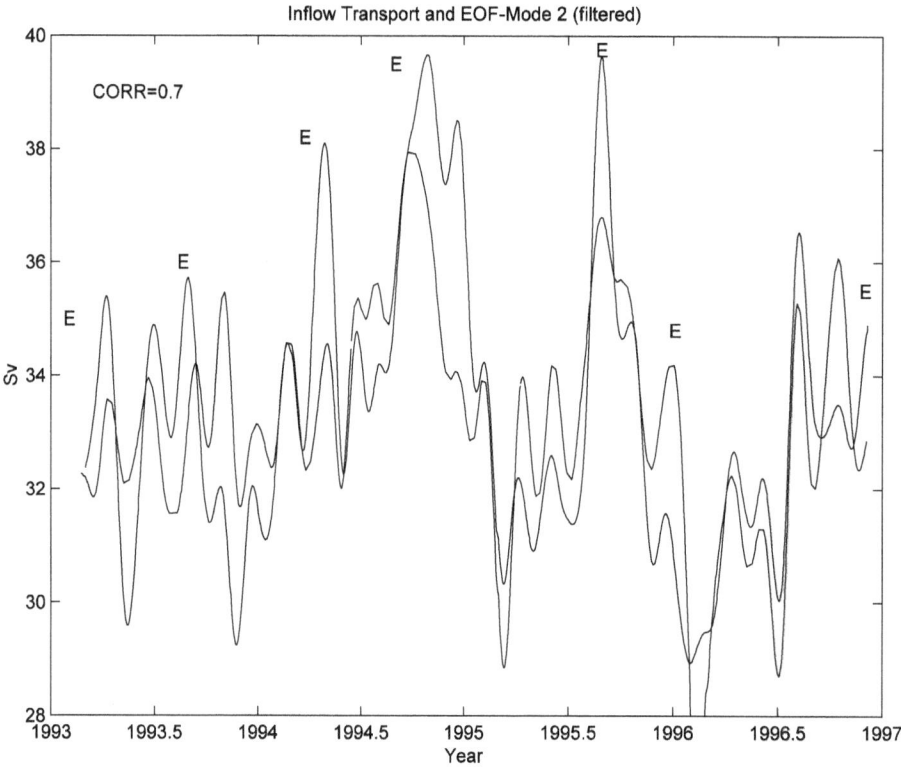

Figure 4.9. Total inflow transport in the upper Yucatan Channel from the Caribbean Sea into the GOM (solid line), the time evolution of EOF mode 2 (dashed line), and eddy shedding events "E" (From Ezer et al., 2003).

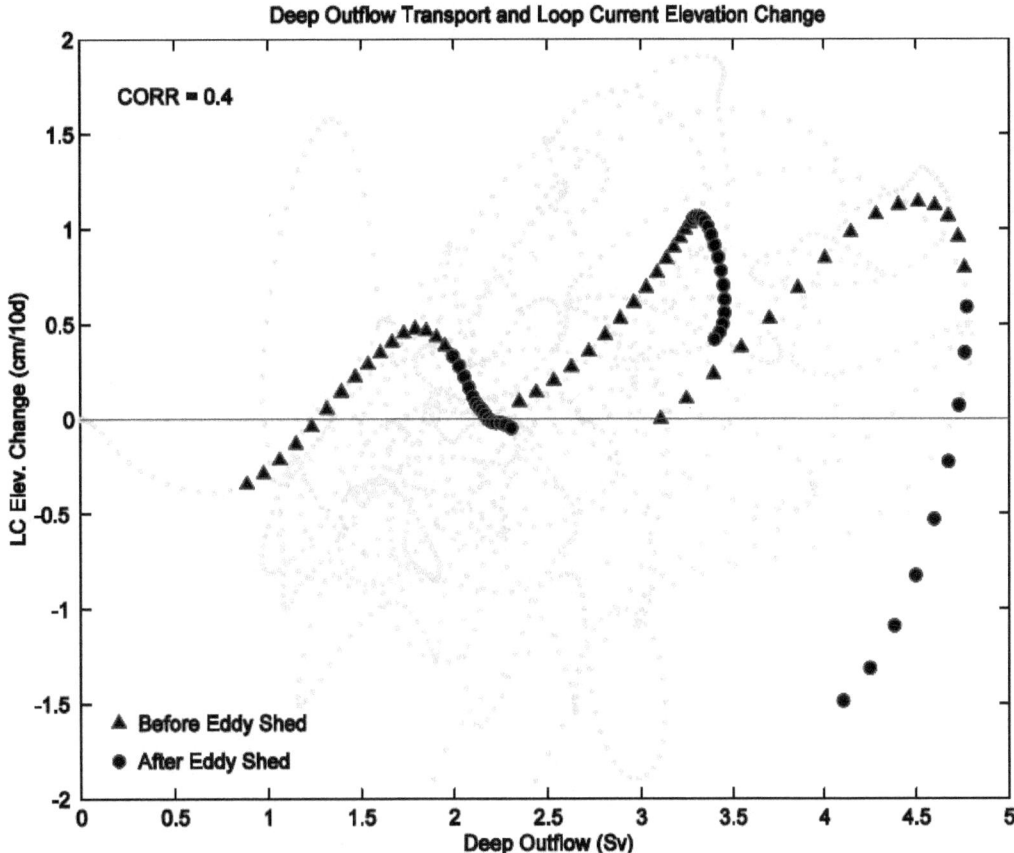

Figure 4.10. Deep outflow (in the POM) from the Gulf below 800 m (x-axis) and the change in sea level in the Loop Current region (positive y-axis values indicate times when the Loop Current is growing in area). The changes in these parameters for three eddies are indicated: blue triangles are for the two weeks before eddy shedding events; circles are for the two weeks afterward. The linear regression coefficient between deep transport and Loop Current change is 0.4 for all daily values, but is 0.7 if only periods around eddy shedding events are considered (from Ezer et al., 2002).

5. RESULTS FROM NUMERICAL MODELING STUDIES USING MICOM

5.1. Miami Isopycnic-Coordinate Ocean Model (MICOM)

Almost all mainstream ocean models in use today are based on the same equations of motion. Different models, however, formulate the solutions in different ways. The Miami model is designed so that the "horizontal" coordinate system follows the slope of the density field of the ocean. This choice does not automatically solve all problems, but its purpose is to

- avoid inconsistencies between vertical and horizontal transport terms that cause (among other things) false diapycnal mixing;

- hide truncation errors associated with horizontal transport behind the smoke screen of isopycnal mixing.

The model is in widespread use in the ocean modeling community and is well described on their home page:

http://oceanmodeling.rsmas.miami.edu/micom/

Some of the results of this study have already been submitted for publication. See, for example, Cherubin et al. (2004) and Romanou et al. (2004).

5.2. General Circulation Patterns in the Gulf of Mexico from MICOM

The upper-layer circulation in the Gulf is, of course, anticyclonic. The main result from the analysis of the MICOM simulation of the horizontal circulation in the Gulf of Mexico is that the circulation is reversed in the deep waters. Figure 5.1 shows the 6-year averaged Eulerian circulation at 400 m; an anticyclonic (clockwise) gyre appears, with two circulation cells in the west. The northern cell is anticyclonic, in part because most of the Loop Current rings end their lifetime in this region. An intense jet is observed on the western side of the anticyclonic gyre. South of this region, the model shows a cylconic circulation cell. Deeper in the Gulf, the dominant feature remains the western jet of the anticyclonic gyre flowing along the shelf slope of the Gulf of Mexico. Figure 5.2 shows a similar view at 900 m.

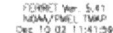

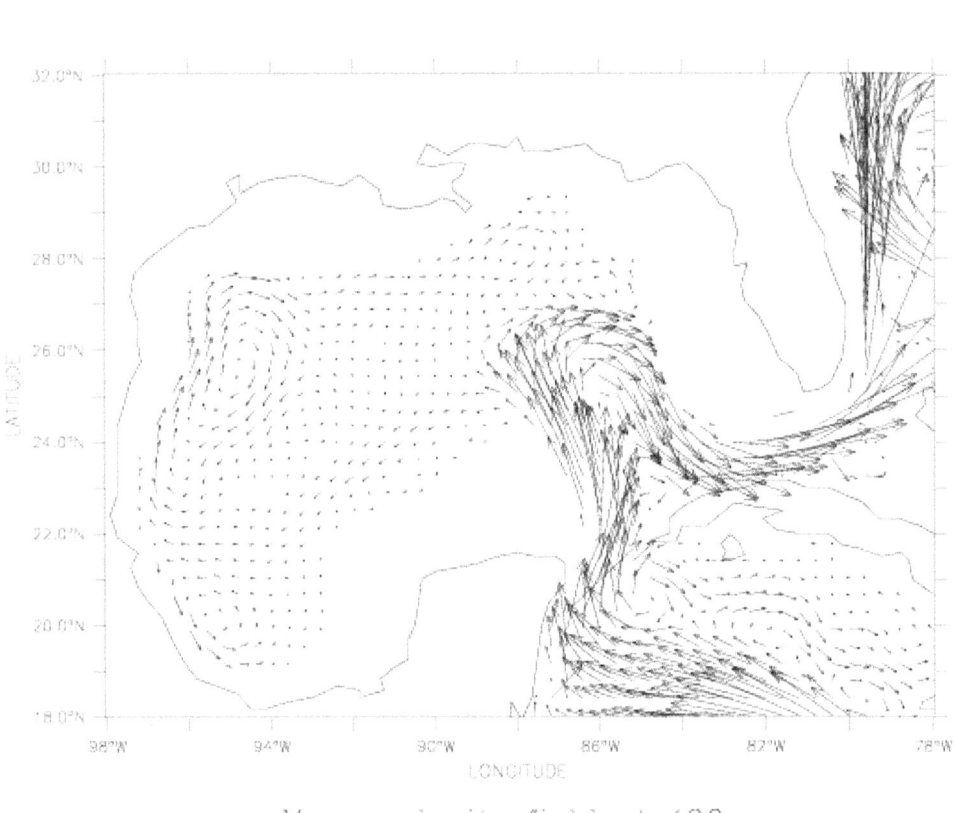

Figure 5.1. Mean velocity field from the MICOM model at a depth of 400 m.

Z (METERS) : -900

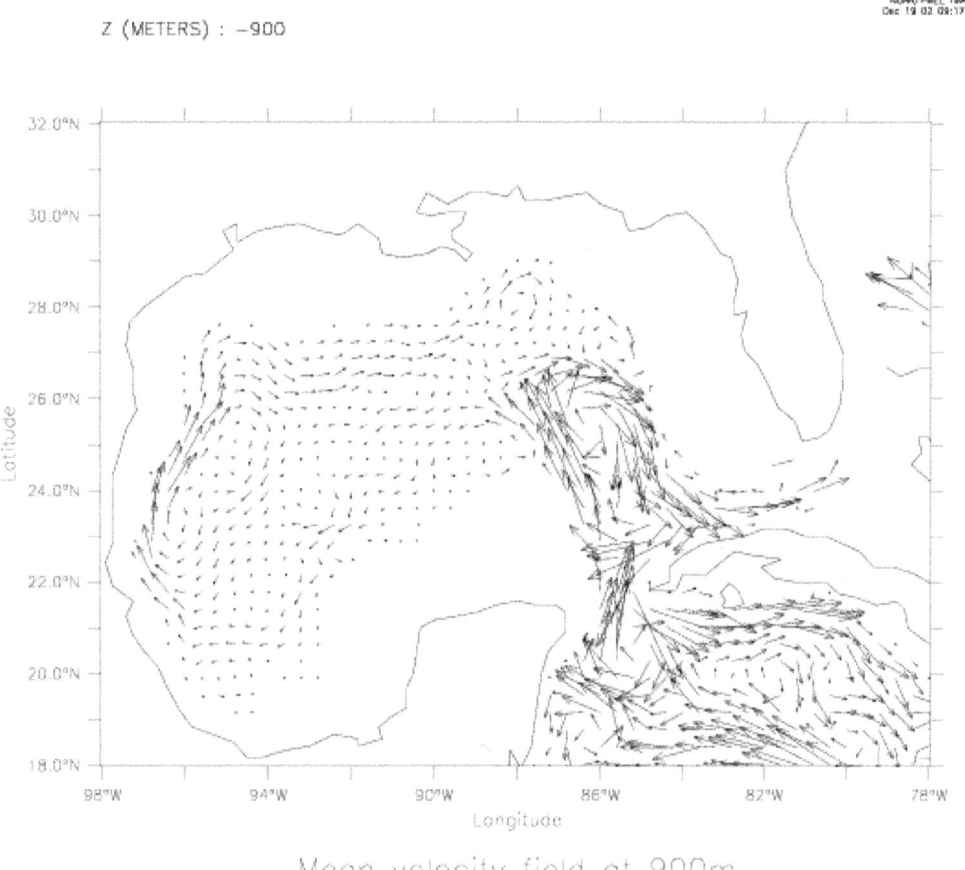

Mean velocity field at 900m
→ 5.00

Figure 5.2. Mean velocity field from the MICOM model at a depth of 900 m.

FERRET Ver. 5.41
NOAA/PMEL TMAP
Dec 10 02 13:28:13

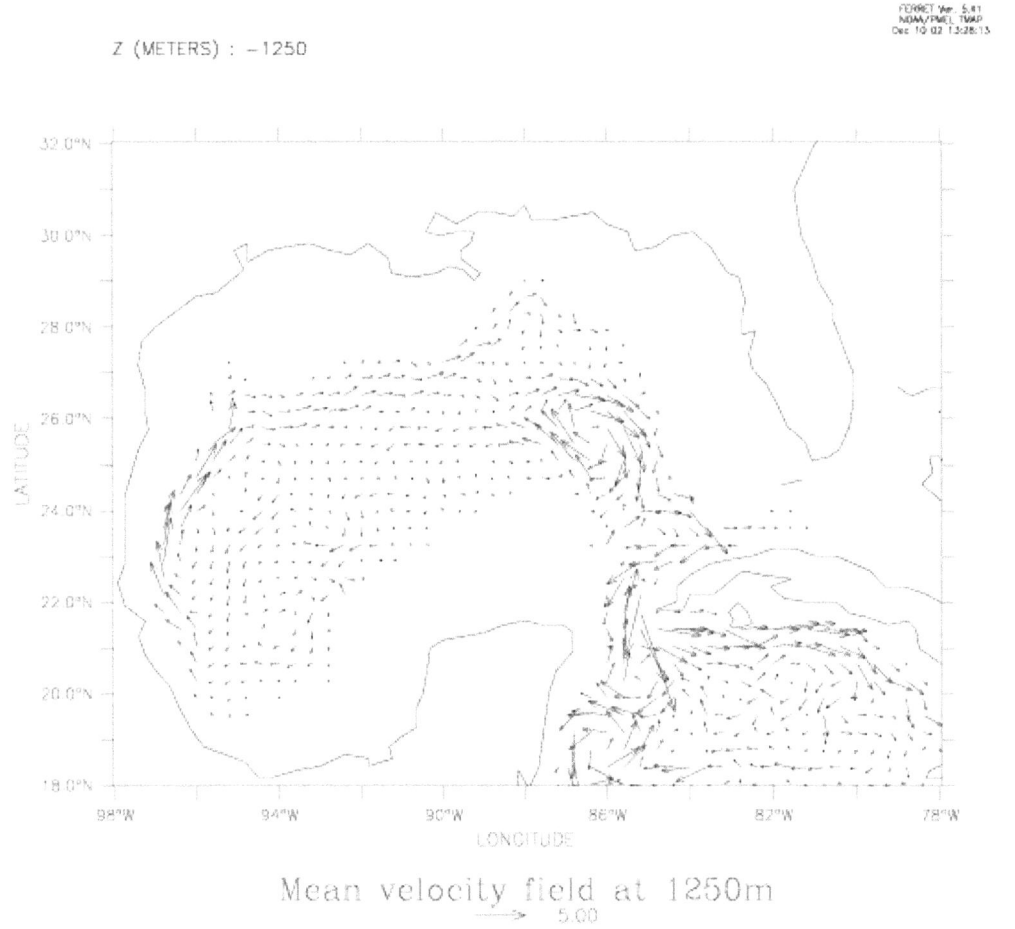

Mean velocity field at 1250m
→ 5.00

Figure 5.3. Mean velocity field from the MICOM model at a depth of 1,250 m.

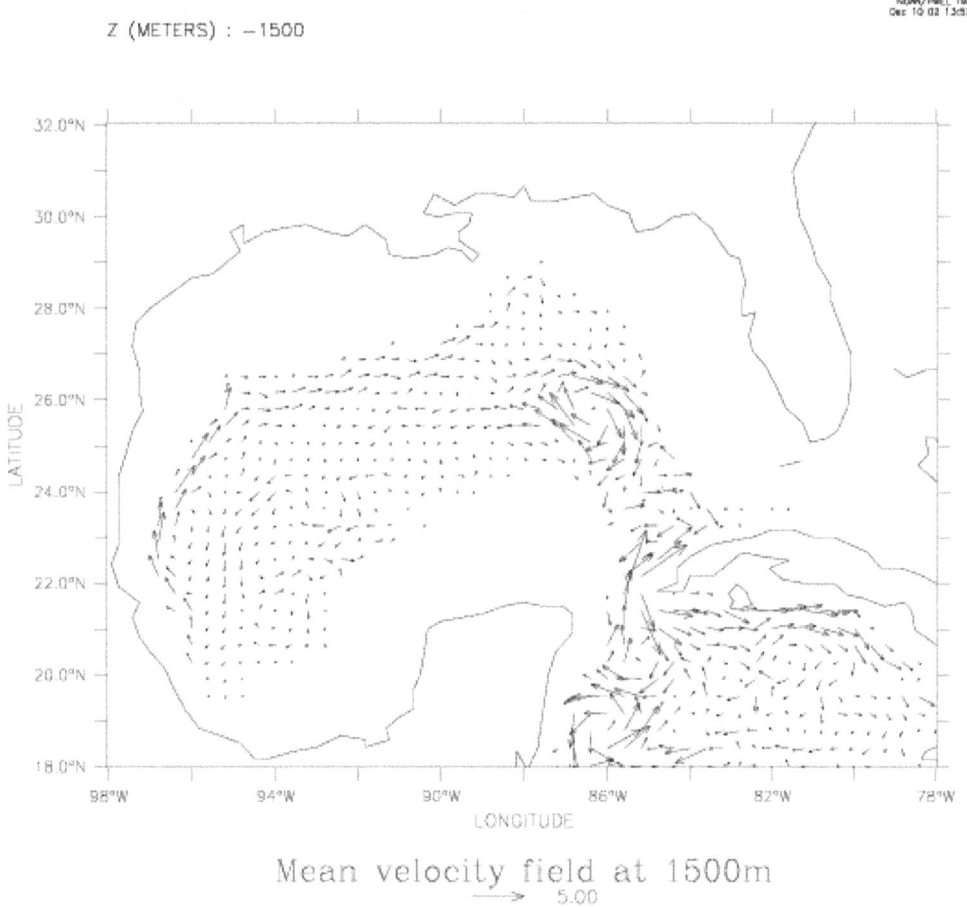

Mean velocity field at 1500m

Figure 5.4. Mean velocity field from the MICOM model at a depth of 1,500 m.

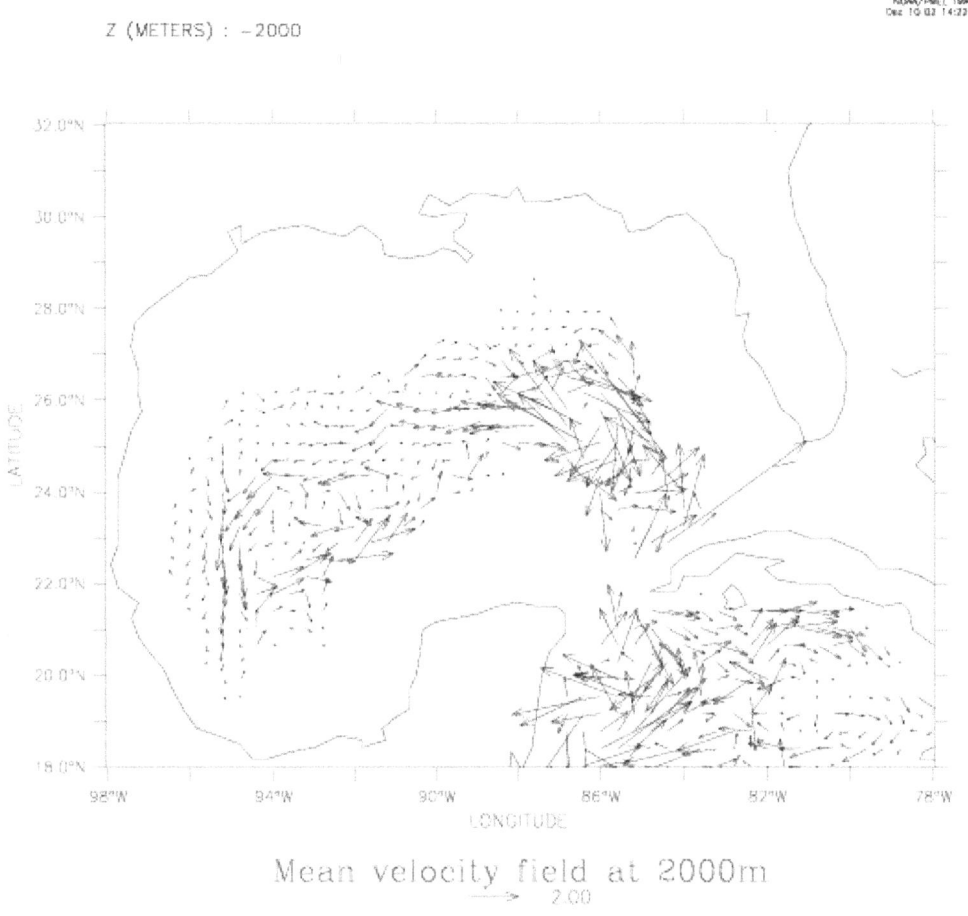

Figure 5.5. Mean velocity field from the MICOM model at a depth of 2,000 m.

On the other hand, the cyclonic circulation cell becomes weaker with depth and has shifted slightly to the east of the south corner of the western Gulf. Figure 5.3 shows the mean flow at 1,250 m, and Figure 5.4 shows the mean flow at 1,500 m. Finally, Figure 5.5 shows that at 2,000 m the dominant circulation is cyclonic. The current is to the west in the deepest part of the Gulf, veers to the east in the western Gulf and flows along the southern shelf slope. North of the cyclonic gyre, a weak anticyclone is still present. In the Loop Current area, the horizontal circulation in these model results is always anticyclonic. This pattern is not the same as found in the Princeton model nor does it agree with observations. We are continuing to study this feature.

While this project has focused on the mean flow around the edges of the deep Gulf, it remains true that the mean flow is not always the topic of greatest interest to some readers (nor one of the most robust features of model results). To show a measure of the energy of the flow, Figure 5.6 shows the standard deviation of the flow at 900 m. Figure 5.7 shows the equivalent standard deviation at 1,500 m. At 900 m the standard deviation ranges from ~2cm/sec in the west to 6 cm/sec beneath the Loop Current. It is clear that these values are as large as the mean flow itself. The means and standard deviation decrease only slightly at 1,500 m and the general conclusion remains the same.

5.3. Strong Current Events Near the Bottom of the Gulf of Mexico

In MICOM simulation, we followed the occurrence of strong current events in the depth range 500-1,500 m on the northern shelf slope of the Gulf of Mexico over six years. The peak speeds in the model are about 28 cm/s between 500 and 600 m and 20 cm/s between 1,300 and 1,600 m. Those events are strongly associated with the generation of Loop Current rings in the eastern Gulf and with its westward motion. This finding is especially clear when these events occur on the northern shelf of the Gulf of Mexico between 90°W and the western gulf. Figures 5.8 and 5.9 show the current bursts using longitude-versus-time diagrams. These plots show their propagation to the west as well as their intensity.

5.4. Meridional Distribution of the Zonal Transport at 90°W

In this section we address the transport budget across a meridional section at 90°W. Somewhat arbitrarily, we divided the section through the middle of the Gulf of Mexico, resulting in a northern and a southern half. The transport budget reveals an anticylonic pattern with more flow going to the east in the northern half and more going to the west in the southern half. All the increases of current transport

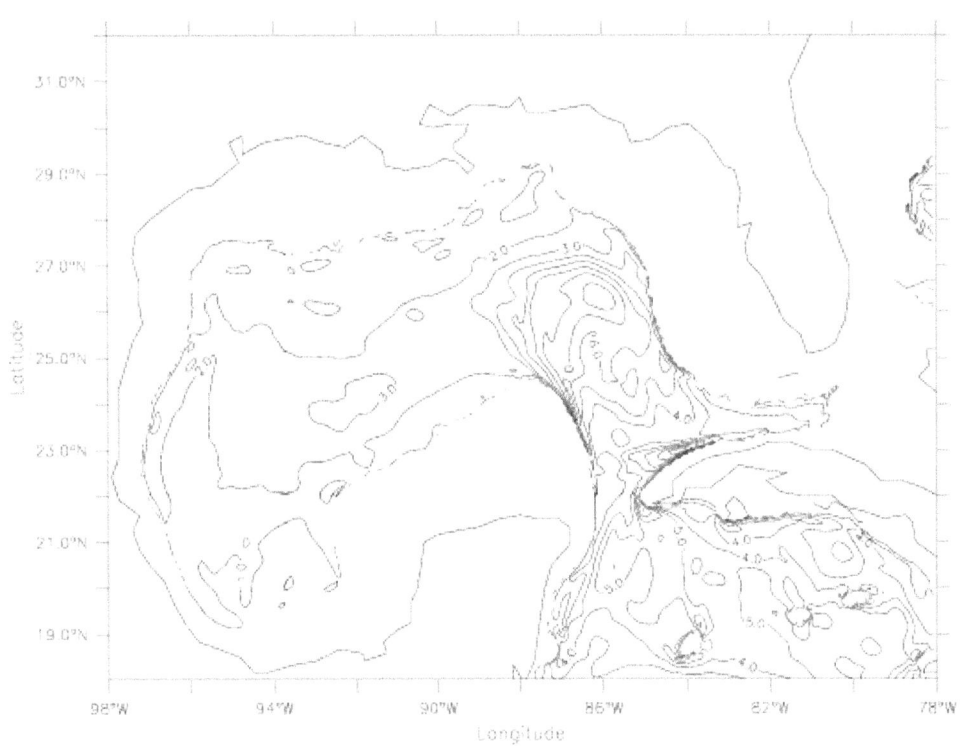

Figure 5.6. Standard deviation of the velocity field at 900 m (see for comparison
Figure 5.2).

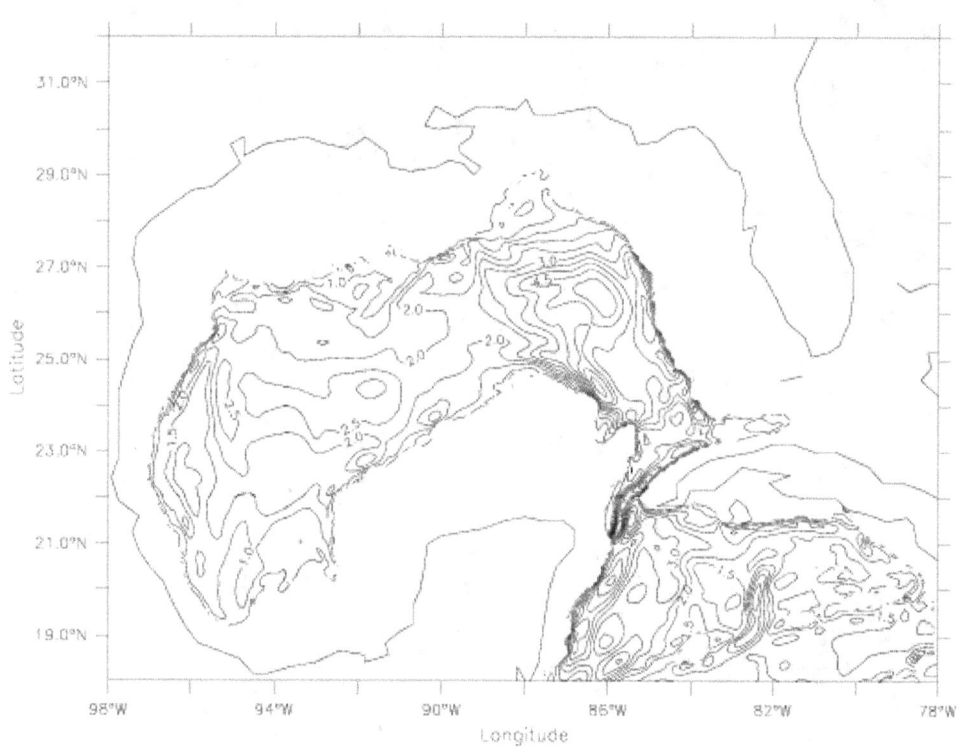

Standard deviation of the mean velocity field at 1500m

Figure 5.7. Standard deviation of the velocity field at 1,500 m.

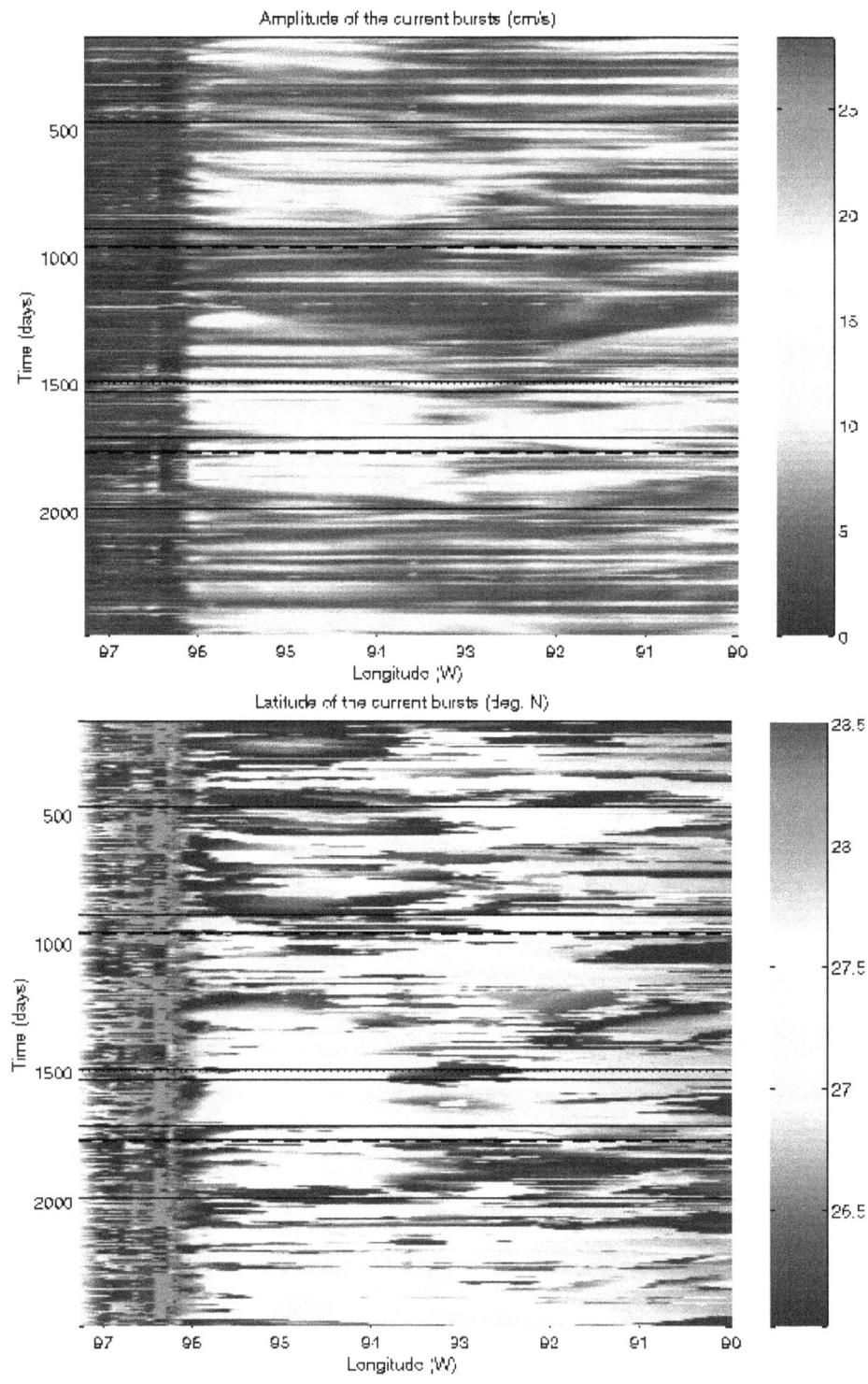

Figure 5.8. Amplitude of current bursts in layer 10, in a latitude-time diagram (upper panel) and the location of the burst (latitude) (lower panel).

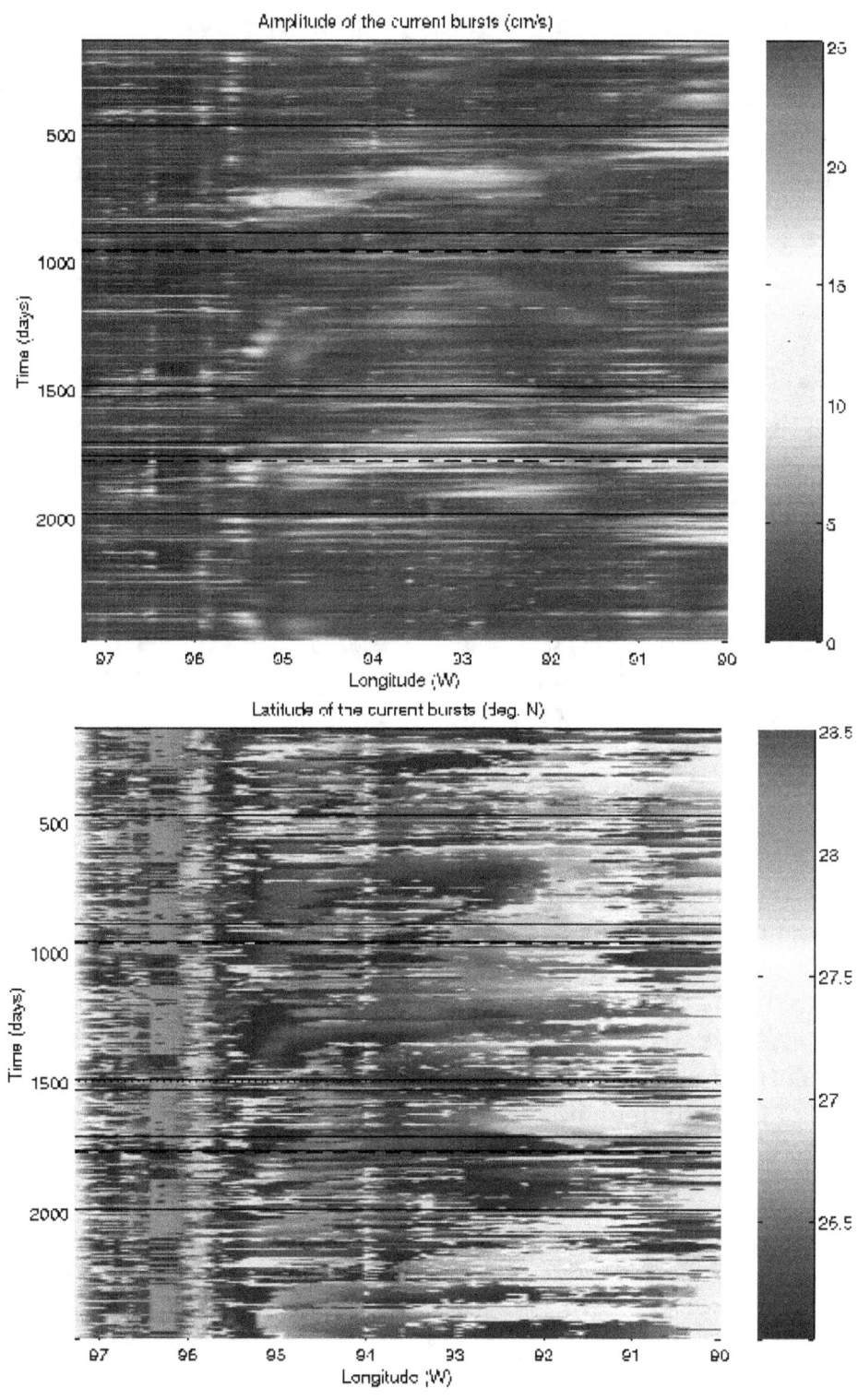

Figure 5.9. Longitude-time plots of the amplitude and the location of strong bursts in layer 13.

in both directions are associated with a Loop current ring passage. During those events, the transport in the deep layers also increases, as shown in Figure 5.10. The budget result gives a weak eastward transport of 0.08 Sv (1 Sv = 10^6 m^3/s), with a weak eastward component above 1,300 m (0.26 Sv) and a westward one below (-0.17 Sv). The paths followed by the water parcels are given by the Lagrangian trajectories as described in the next section.

5.5. Lagrangian Trajectories in the Deep Gulf Circulation

One of the goals of this study was to determine whether some of the Gulf of Mexico waters have a net transport returning to the Caribbean Sea below the depth of the sill in the Florida Strait. The previous results showed a strong eastward transport in the northern half of the Gulf; the Eulerian currents between 1,000 and 2,000 m suggest a return flow from the north to the Caribbean Sea (Figures 5.3 and 5.4). Figure 5.11 shows a collection of Lagrangian trajectories in layer 13 of the model. Layer 13 occupies the depth range ~900-1,400 m in the Yucatan Channel. We see that the water parcels that return to the Caribbean Sea come from the northern Gulf in a region located east of a ring that has recently separated. These trajectories were obtained as the Loop Current ring was moving to the west and the path of the Loop Current was going straight from the Caribbean Sea out through the Florida Straits. In the model no flow beneath layer 13 was observed to return to the Caribbean Sea just after a Loop Current ring formation.

Finally, we examine the model Lagrangian trajectories in the intermediate layers, between 400 and 1,000 m. These trajectories reveal new patterns of the circulation not visible in the above circulation vector plots. Because of the cyclones generated during the formation of a Loop Current ring, some water parcels can be entrained against the main stream. Therefore, instead of following the anticyclonic gyre described above, the water parcels undergo a cyclonic motion initiated east of a Loop Current ring in the eastern Gulf. Figure 5.12 shows particles that drift to the southwest and then return to the east. Those very surprising motions are similar to those that have been observed in actual float trajectories.

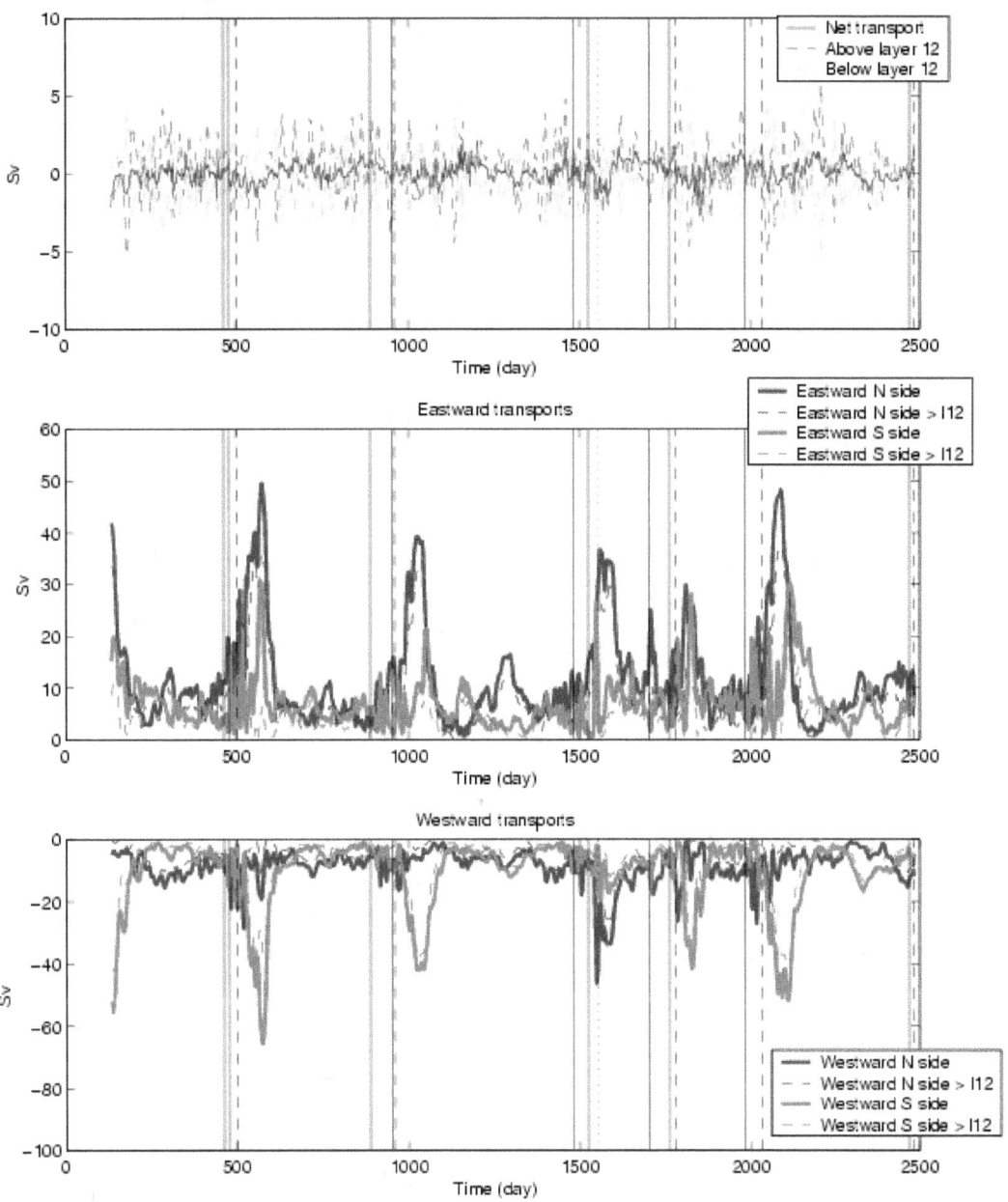

Figure 5.10. Time series of transports across a N-S section at 90°W. Top panel shows transports above and below layer 12 (approximately 1,300 m). Lower two panels show transports to the east and to the west, in the northern and southern halves of the section.

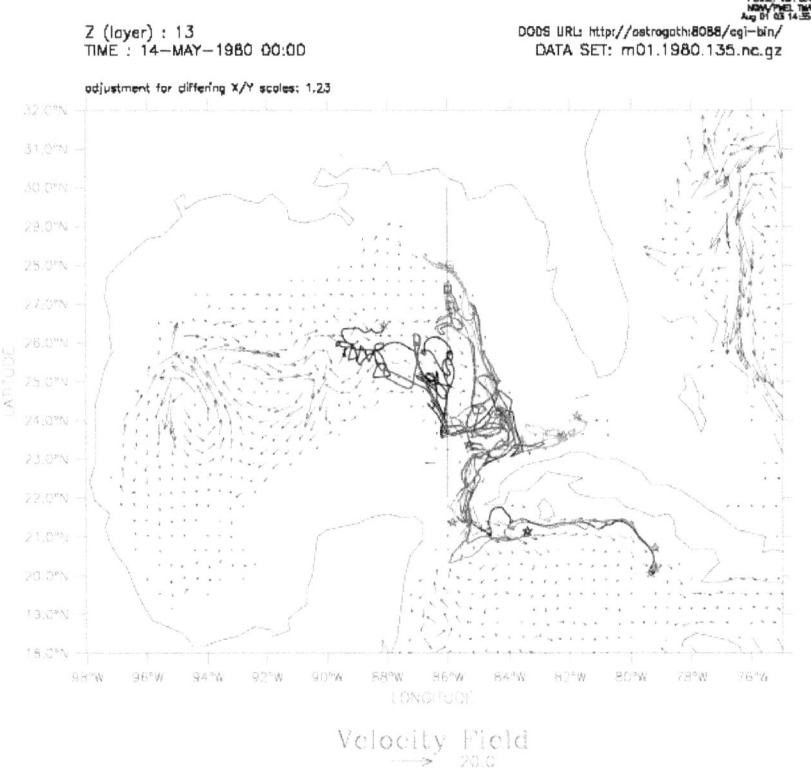

Figure 5.11. Lagrangian trajectories of particles in layer 13, originating in the northern and central regions of the Gulf. The particles are launched along the red N-S line at the squares; the end points of the paths are shown by the stars.

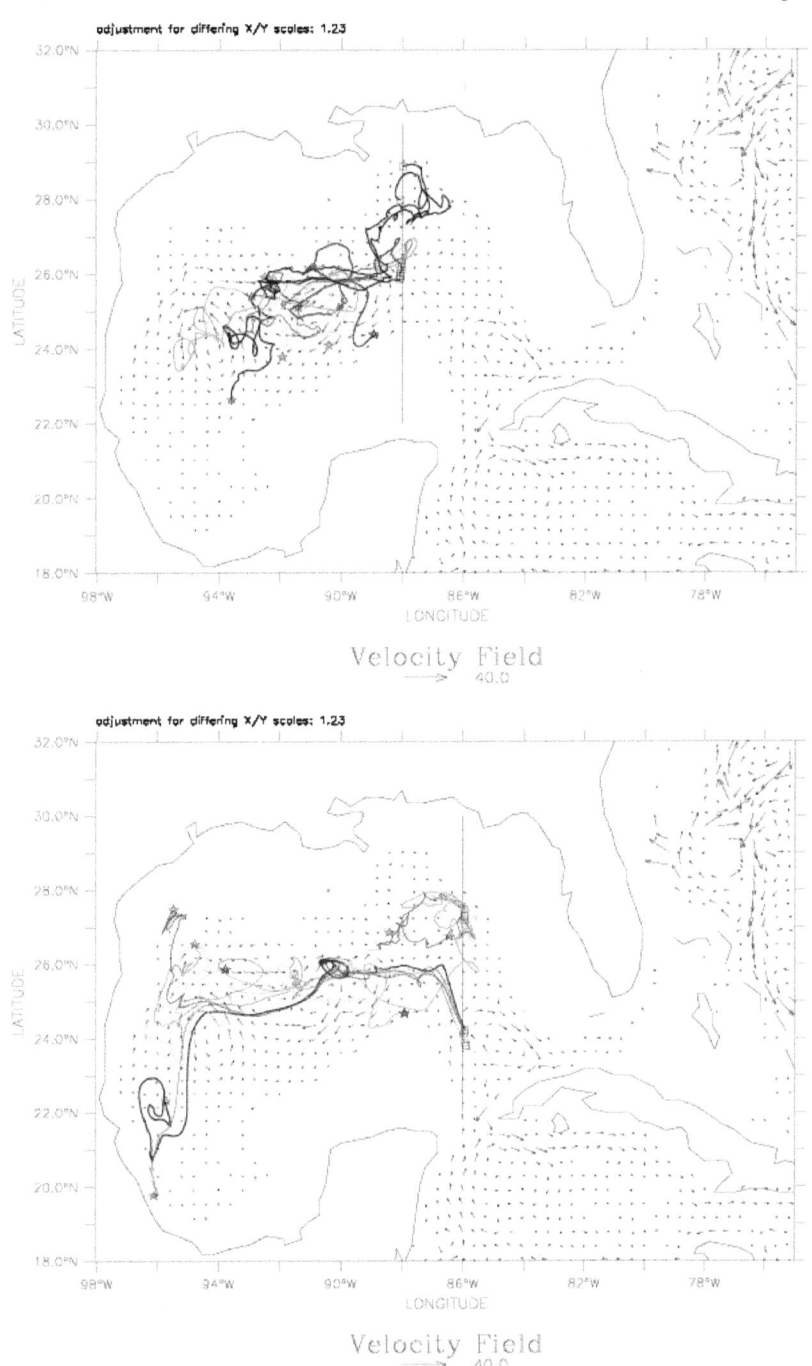

Figure 5.12. Lagrangian trajectories in layer 12 for two different time intervals. The particles are launched along the red N-S line at the squares; the end points of the paths are shown by the stars; see text.

67

6. ANNOTATED BIBLIOGRAPHY

The following is a brief discussion of publications resulting from MMS support of this project.

Cherubin, L.M, W. Sturges, and E. Chassignet, 2004. Deep flow variability in the vicinity of the Yucatan Straits from a high resolution MICOM simulation. *J. Geophys Res., submitted.*

The deep flow variability in the vicinity of the Yucatan Channel between the Caribbean Sea and the Gulf of Mexico is examined within a high resolution numerical simulation of the North Atlantic Ocean. First, since the model is forced with daily ECMWF forcing, the circulation in the vicinity of the Yucatan channel presents a high variability in the flow regimes and in the shedding period which is in good agreement with earlier observations. The outflow (towards the Carribean Sea) in the Yucatan Channel is shown to be in part controlled by the regular east-west shift of the core of the Loop Current in phase with the transport variations. The outflow is shown to compensate the excess of inflow whatever the Loop Current extension. The analysis of the growth of the loop is also shown to be in good agreement with the retroflexion paradox and with the ballooning process proposed by Pichevin and Nof (1997) and Nof and Pichevin (2001) to explain the Loop Current Ring formation. Moreover, at the end of each cycle of Loop Current ring formation a sudden deepening of the loop occurs together with an intensification of the transport and the currents in the deep layers underneath the Loop Current. This process is shown to be connected with the growth of an instability, probably barotropic, as originally proposed by Hurlburt and Thompson.

Cherubin, L.M., Y. Morel and E. Chassignet, 2004. Loop Current ring formation: a new mechanism. To be submitted to *J. Phys Oceanogr.*

The formation of the Loop Current rings is studied by comparing the growth of cyclones around the Loop Current ring, during its formation stage, in the very high resolution MICOM simulation with a case study model. In this case study ring; and those cyclones are responsible for the cleavage between the Loop Current ring and the Loop Current itself. Secondly, the Campeche bank forces the mode 3 instability (3 growing cyclones) of the Loop Current ring. The steady state is a pentapole, which consists in an anticyclone surrounded by four cyclones. Thirdly, the slope of the northern Gulf compensates the beta effect what prevents the instability to grow as a mode 1 which produces only one big cyclone north of the anticyclone.

DeHaan, Christopher J., 2002. Determining the Deep Current Structure in the Gulf of Mexico and the Yucatan Strait from Multiple Data Types.

Doctoral Dissertation, Dept. of Oceanography, Florida State University, Tallahassee. October, 2002. This Dissertation is the basis of the journal article described below. Dr. DeHaan is now an oceanographer at the U.S. Navy Oceanographic Office, Stennis MS.

DeHaan, C.J., and W. Sturges, 2004. Deep cyclonic circulation in the Gulf of Mexico. *J. Phys Oceanogr. in press.*

This paper examines the historical density field of the Gulf as well as all the available (non-proprietary) direct current observations. Using moored current meter data and deep drifting floats, they conclude that the deep (~2000 m) flow around the edges of the Gulf is cyclonic. Section III of this report is based heavily on this paper.

Ezer, T., L.-Y. Oey. and H.-C. Lee, 2002. Simulation of velocities in the Yucatan Channel, In: Proc., Oceans 2002, MTS/IEEE Publ., 1467-1471.

Results from the POM numerical simulations of the Gulf of Mexico are shown to compare very well with past and recent observations of velocities and transports in the Yucatan Channel. The main model inflow into the Gulf is found near the surface in the western part of the Channel, while return flows back into the Caribbean Sea are found near the surface on the eastern side of the Channel and along the eastern and western slopes around 1500 m depth. The location and transport of each one of these flows are in good agreement with recent observations (Ochoa et al., 2001). Variations in the upper inflow and deep outflow transports seem to correlate with variations in the extension of the Loop Current, as suggested by analyses of observations (Bunge et al., 2002) . Such correlations were found to be especially high near the time when Loop Current eddies are shed into the Gulf of Mexico and return deep transports out of the Gulf are significantly larger.

70

Ezer, T., L.-Y. Oey, H.-C. Lee, and W. Sturges, 2003. The variability of currents in the Yucatan Channel: Analysis of results from a numerical ocean model, *J. Geophys. Res.*, *108*, 3012, 10.1029/2002JC001509.

An Empirical Orthogonal Function (EOF) analysis helps to identify, possibly for the first time, the physical parameters responsible for the dominant modal fluctuations in the Yucatan Channel and the likely reason for the model eddy shedding periods. The EOF mode 1 and mode 2 represent the variations in cross-channel oscillations and in inflow transport into the Gulf, respectively. The third and fourth EOF modes together, represent variations in the deep current over the sill, with long periods similar to those observed by Maul et al. (1985). The dominant EOF modal periods, around 6, 8 and 11 months are almost identical to the most dominant observed periods of Loop Current eddy shedding found by Sturges and Leben (2000). A follow up study by Oey et al. (2003b) provides further analysis of the effect of wind variations and Caribbean eddies on the eddy shedding frequency and mechanism.

Romanou, Anastasia, Eric P. Chassignet, and Wilton Sturges, 2004. The Gulf of Mexico circulation within a high-resolution numerical simulation of the North Atlantic. *J. Geophys. Res.*, *109*, C01003, doi:10.1029/2003JC001770.

This paper was written while Ms. Romanou worked with Chassignet. It reports the results of the MICOM studies over the full Gulf. The characteristics of rings (size, lifetimes, etc.) are compared with observations. There is also a discussion of comparisons of flow in Yucatan Channel with the observations of the Ensenada group. Ms. Romanou then went to a post-doctoral position at N.Y.U.

Wang, D.-P., L.-Y. Oey, T. Ezer, and P. Hamilton, 2003. Near-surface currents in DeSoto Canyon (1997-99): Comparison of current meters, satellite observation and model simulation, *J. Phys. Oceanogr.*, 33(1), 313-326.

This paper was the result of several MMS projects, including the Gulf of Mexico deep flows collaborative study by Ezer-Sturges, the Gulf of Mexico deep flows and energetics study by Oey and collaborators, and the GOM hindcast system development efforts by Oey-Ezer. In this paper, the data assimilation methodology, previously developed for the Gulf Stream region (Ezer and Mellor, 1994, 1997), has been evaluated for the Gulf. The model's hindcasts are compared with analysis of moored current meter data in DeSoto Canyon and with analysis of altimeter data, using the Singular Value Decomposition (SVD) method. The model results were found to compare well with the mean and variance of the currents in the Canyon, which seem to be largely influenced by the local topography.

7. REFERENCES

Bunge, L., J. Ochoa, A. Badan, J. Candela, and J. Sheinbaum. 2002. Deep flows in the Yucatan Channel and their relation to changes in the Loop Current extension. *J. Geophys. Res.*, 107: 10.1029/2001 JC001256.

Blumberg, A. F. and G. L. Mellor. 1987. A description of a three-dimensional coastal ocean circulation model, *in* Three-Dimensional Coastal Ocean Models, Coastal and Estuarine Stud., vol. 4, edited by N. S. Heaps, pp. 1-16, Amer. Geophys. U., Washington, D.C.

Cherubin, L.M., W. Sturges, and E. Chassignet. 2004. Deep flow variability in the vicinity of the Yucatan Straits from a high resolution MICOM simulation. *J. Geophys Res*. Submitted.

Conkright, M. E., S. Levitus, T. O'Brien, T. P. Boyer, C. Stephens, D. Johnson, O. Baranova, J. Antonov, R. Gelfield, J. Rochester, and C. Forgy. 2000. World ocean database 1998. Technical Report, Ocean Climate Laboratory, National Oceanographic Data Center, NOAA, Washington D.C.

Davis, R. E., D. C. Webb, L. A. Regier, and J. Dufour. 1991. The Autonomous Lagrangian Circulation Explorer (ALACE). *J. Atmos. Ocean. Techn.*, 9:264-285.

DeHaan, C.J. and W. Sturges. 2004. Deep cyclonic circulation in the Gulf of Mexico. *J. Phys Oceanogr*. In press.

Ezer, T. and G. L. Mellor. 1994. Continuous assimilation of GEOSAT altimeter data into a three-dimensional primitive equation Gulf Stream model, *J. Phys. Oceanogr.*, 24: 832-847.

Ezer,T. and G. L. Mellor. 1997. Data assimilation experiments in the Gulf Stream region: How useful are satellite-derived surface data for nowcasting the subsurface fields?, *J. Atmos. Ocean Tech.*, 14(6): 1379-1391.

Ezer, T., L.-Y. Oey, and H.-C. Lee. 2002. Simulation of velocities in the Yucatan Channel, In: Proc., Oceans 2002, MTS/IEEE Publ., 1467-1471.

Ezer, T., L.-Y. Oey, H.-C. Lee, and W. Sturges. 2003. The variability of currents in the Yucatan Channel: Analysis of results from a numerical ocean model, *J. Geophys. Res.*, 108(C1): 3012, 10.1029/2002JC001509.

Girton, J. B. and T. B. Sanford. 2003. Descent and modification of the overflow plume in the Denmark Strait. *J. Phys. Oceanogr.*, 33: 1351-1364.

Hamilton, P. 1990. Deep currents in the Gulf of Mexico, *J. Phys. Oceanogr.*, 20: 1087-1104.

Hamilton, P. and A. Lugo-Fernandez. 2001. Observations of high-speed deep currents in the northern Gulf of Mexico. *Geophys. Res. Lett*, 28: 2867-2870.

Hofmann, E. E. and S. J. Worley. 1986. An investigation of the circulation of the Gulf of Mexico. *J. Geophys. Res.*, 91(C12): 14,221-14,236.

Maul, G. A., D. A. Mayer, and S. R. Baig. 1985. Comparisons between a continuous 3-year current-meter observation at the sill of the Yucatan Strait, satellite measurements of Loop Current area, and regional sea level. *J. Geophys. Res.*, 90: 9089-9096.

Molinari, R. L. and D. Mayer. 1980. Physical oceanographic conditions at a potential OTEC site in the Gulf of Mexico; 27.5°N, 85.5°W, NOAA Tech. Memo. ERL-AOML - 42; AOML, NOAA, Miami, FL, May 1980.

Molinari, R. L., J. F. Festa, and D. W. Behringer. 1978. The circulation in the Gulf of Mexico derived from estimated dynamic height fields. *J. Phys. Oceanogr.*, 8: 987-996.

Nof, D. and T. Pichevin. 2001. The ballooning of outflows. *J. Phys Oceanogr.*, 31: 3045-3058.

Niiler, P. P. and W. S. Richardson. 1973. Seasonal variability of the Florida Current. *J. Mar. Res.*, 31(3): 144-167.

Ochoa, J., J. Sheinbaum, A. Badan, J. Candela, and D. Wilson. 2001. Geostrophy via potential vorticity inversion in the in the Yucatan Channel. *J. Mar. Res.*, 59:725-747.

Oey, L.-Y., H.C. Lee, T. Fan, T. Ezer, H. Wei, and P. Hamilton. 2004. A model hindcast of the circulation in the Gulf of Mexico. Manuscript in preparation.

Oey, L.-Y., P. Hamilton, and H.-C. Lee. 2003a. Modeling and data analyses of circulation processes in the Gulf of Mexico: Final report. U.S. Dept. of the Interior, Minerals Management Service, Gulf of Mexico OCS Region, New Orleans, LA. OCS Study MMS 2003-074.

Oey, L.-Y., H. C. Lee, and W.J. Schmitz, Jr. 2003b. Effects of winds and Caribbean eddies on the frequency of Loop Current eddy shedding: A numerical model study. *J. Geophy. Res.* 108(C10): 3324, doi:10.1029/2002JC001698.

Oey, L.-Y. and H.-C. Lee. 2002. Deep eddy energy and topographic Rossby waves in the Gulf of Mexico. *J. Phys. Oceanogr.*, 32: 2499-3527.

Pichevin, T. and D. Nof. 1997. The momentum imbalance paradox. *Tellus,* 49A:298-319.

Romanou, A., E. P. Chassignet, and W. Sturges. 2004. The Gulf of Mexico circulation within a high-resolution numerical simulation of the North Atlantic. *J. Geophys. Res.* 109: C01003, doi:10.1029/2003JC001770.

Schmitz, W. J., Jr. and P. L. Richardson. 1991. On the sources of the Florida Current, *Deep-Sea Res.*, 38 (Suppl. 1): S379-S409.

Sheinbaum, J., J. Candela, A. Badan, and J. Ochoa. 2002. Flow structure and transport in the Yucatan Channel. *Geophys. Res. Lett.*, 29: 1-4.

Spall, M. A. and J. E. Price. 1998. Mesoscale variability in Denmark Strait: The PV outflow hypothesis. *J. of Phys. Oceanogr.*, 28: 1598-1623.

Sturges, W. and R. Leben. 2000. Frequency of ring separations from the Loop Current in the Gulf of Mexico: A revised estimate. *J. Phys. Oceanogr.,* 30: 1,814-1,818.

Wang, D.-P., L.-Y. Oey, T. Ezer, and P. Hamilton. 2003. Near-surface currents in DeSoto Canyon (1997-99): Comparison of current meters, satellite observation and model simulation. *J. Phys. Oceanogr.*, 33(1): 313-326.

Weatherly, G. L. and N. Wienders. 2004. Mean circulation in the Gulf of Mexico at 900 m from PALACE floats. *J. Geophys. Res.* Submitted.

Wienders, N., G. L. Weatherly, and S. E. Welsh. 2002. Gulf of Mexico 900-meter circulation from PALACE floats. Abstract, EOS, *Proceedings Amer. Geophys. Union.*

The Department of the Interior Mission

As the Nation's principal conservation agency, the Department of the Interior has responsibility for most of our nationally owned public lands and natural resources. This includes fostering sound use of our land and water resources; protecting our fish, wildlife, and biological diversity; preserving the environmental and cultural values of our national parks and historical places; and providing for the enjoyment of life through outdoor recreation. The Department assesses our energy and mineral resources and works to ensure that their development is in the best interests of all our people by encouraging stewardship and citizen participation in their care. The Department also has a major responsibility for American Indian reservation communities and for people who live in island territories under U.S. administration.

The Minerals Management Service Mission

As a bureau of the Department of the Interior, the Minerals Management Service's (MMS) primary responsibilities are to manage the mineral resources located on the Nation's Outer Continental Shelf (OCS), collect revenue from the Federal OCS and onshore Federal and Indian lands, and distribute those revenues.

Moreover, in working to meet its responsibilities, the **Offshore Minerals Management Program** administers the OCS competitive leasing program and oversees the safe and environmentally sound exploration and production of our Nation's offshore natural gas, oil and other mineral resources. The MMS **Minerals Revenue Management** meets its responsibilities by ensuring the efficient, timely and accurate collection and disbursement of revenue from mineral leasing and production due to Indian tribes and allottees, States and the U.S. Treasury.

The MMS strives to fulfill its responsibilities through the general guiding principles of: (1) being responsive to the public's concerns and interests by maintaining a dialogue with all potentially affected parties and (2) carrying out its programs with an emphasis on working to enhance the quality of life for all Americans by lending MMS assistance and expertise to economic development and environmental protection.

www.ingramcontent.com/pod-product-compliance
Lightning Source LLC
Chambersburg PA
CBHW052006280526
45793CB00005B/870